Holding
Accountability
Accountable

What Ought to
Matter in Public Education

KENNETH A. SIROTNIK

Editor

Teachers College, Columbia University
New York and London

Published by Teachers College Press, 1234 Amsterdam Avenue, New York, NY 10027

Library of Congress Cataloging-in-Publication Data

Holding accountability accountable: what ought to matter in public education / Kenneth A. Sirotnik, editor.
   p. cm. -- (Series on school reform)
   Includes bibliographical references and index.
   ISBN 0-8077-4465-4--ISBN 0-8077-4464-6 (pbk.)
   1. Educational accountability — United States. 2. Public schools — United States. I. Sirotnik, Kenneth A. II. Series.

   LB2806.22.H65 2004
   379.1'58--dc22   2003066895

ISBN 0-8077-4464-6 (paper)
ISBN 0-8077-4465-4 (cloth)

the series on school reform

| Patricia A. Wasley | Ann Lieberman | Joseph P. McDonald |
| University of Washington | Carnegie Foundation for the Advancement of Teaching | New York University |

SERIES EDITORS

(Continued)

the series on school reform, *continued*

Kenneth Sirotnik died on January 29, 2004, at the age of 61, following a brief struggle with cancer. He had completed most of the work on this book at the time of his death. In sorrow and sadness, the publisher and the contributors dedicate this book to his memory.

Contents

8 Responsible Accountability and Teacher Learning   135
Patricia A. Wasley

Conclusion Holding Accountability Accountable —
Hope for the Future?   148
Kenneth A. Sirotnik

Acknowledgments

This work would not have been possible without funding from The Rockefeller Foundation and the support from Fred Frelow of the foundation. The foundation, however, does not necessarily endorse the views expressed in this book. I also wish to thank the editors and staff at Teachers College Press for their willingness to publish this work, and for their editorial support in bringing it to print. Many thanks also go to my immediate colleagues on Project PRAISE (Promoting Responsible Accountability in Schools and Education) — Paul Heckman, Roger Soder, and Pat Wasley; and to many other colleagues in the College of Education who have provoked my thinking and fed me many relevant articles and web site addresses over the past several years. And finally, I express my thanks to my research assistant Shawn Olsen-Brown and to two talented undergraduate students, Zach Savich and Judy Yee, for their assistance on various phases of the project.

Critical Concerns About Accountability Concepts and Practices

Kenneth A. Sirotnik

January 9, 2003

Dear Ken,

I was visiting Susan Ohanian's web site after our talk, and I saw the following quote: "It is the greatest of all mistakes to do nothing because you can only do a little. Do what you can." (Sydney Smith)

I have reconsidered taking that other job in the private sector after reading that quote. Unless you happen to be in a classroom at this time, it is impossible to describe how awful the environment is. The testing mania is so pervasive that I feel that my contribution in the next few decades will be minimal, if not zero. Should I continue in education, knowing that my ability to contribute will be negligible?

Another thing that concerns me is that in the current environment, the worst teachers are the ones who appear to be doing the best job. Those who refuse to teach to the test are seen as the worst teachers, because their students won't be prepared to score highly. Do you think teachers such as me will remain in education, given the current climate? Do you know how frustrating it is to know that you are doing a better job than everyone else, but that they are getting evaluated as a better teacher?

The teacher I am replacing has got to be the worst teacher I have

1

ever seen. I had a chance to observe her in class for a week or so, and I was horrified. She knows little math, and is unable to help students appreciate the applications and beauty of math, and so students resort to memorization to pass her moronic tests. The students are so screwed up mathematically that even being here two months, I am still confused as to the proper course to follow. My conscience cannot allow me to imitate her method, even though it is clear that the students and the administrators wish that I would. Most of the students think she was a great teacher. I know why. She expects little, tells them exactly what will be on the test, and they all get great grades, even though they learn absolutely nothing. She is the prototypical bad teacher that we read about, and the one we always say should not be in the classroom.

But here's the irony, Ken. The administration loves her! The parents love her! The students love her! The administration loves her, because she keeps the test scores high. The parents love her because the students are happy. The students love her because it's easy to get a good grade. But the students learn nothing. (There are some exceptions. Some of the students resent the poor teaching, and know that they are screwed mathematically when they go to college. They are glad that I came.)

There are other teachers in this high school that are equally awful and they do a terrible job. They are blissfully unaware of their incompetence, so they can be excused. But many teachers out there know they are doing a lousy job, but simply don't care. They are the real traitors to education. I had some of the students from this school when I taught at the University, and I am beginning to understand why they were so poorly prepared. One of the students in my calculus class passed the placement test, but could not add fractions!

When I ask the students to participate and discover at least some things on their own, or ask them to solve challenging problems, they are confused and angry. They want me to spoon feed them, and ask me for things to memorize so that they can get a good grade on the tests. The superintendent is furious with me, and the principal has asked me to concentrate on preparing the students for the tests, which I refuse to do. The parents are next, and I am the subject of discussion in the community. Some have heard of my methods and want me fired.

When I came to the UW in Seattle, I sacrificed a great deal. I turned my whole life upside down. My family was separated from me for a time, my financial situation was affected, and has still not recovered, and I lost 3 or four years of my career. Now I find that, after having made monumental efforts to improve my teaching skills, that my services are much less valuable now! I am doing a better job, but I am judged to be a poor teacher. Those who are doing an awful job are judged to be doing an excellent job.

How can I go on knowing that doing a good job will cause me to be evaluated poorly? How can I watch other teachers do a terrible job and get excellent evaluations? Where does that leave me? How can anything ever change when the people who evaluate me are unable to recognize a good teacher? The administration here wouldn't know a good teacher if it came up and bit them on the ass. How am I expected to do a good job if I am not recognized for doing so? Is that humanly possible for an extended period of time?

One answer is that I can prepare other teachers. But if I reach them in my classes, and they understand what doing a good job really is, aren't I condemning them to being treated as I currently am? Would it not be better to tell them the truth, that they are likely to be evaluated as excellent if they teach "Parrot Math?" I can not and will not do that. So what is left? And think about George W's Leave No Child Behind act. We know the testing mania is going to get worse. How can I prepare good teachers in this climate?

If you think about the situation long enough, you realize the only answer. The only logical way to proceed is to pretend like you are teaching parrot math, make sure the students are prepared for those idiotic tests, but then surreptitiously try and do some good when no one is watching. In other words, like the opening quote, I can do a little. But knowing that I am being prevented from doing a lot is frustrating me beyond belief. Can my conscience allow me to do a lousy job most of the time, just so that I can do a good job some of the time? Such a superhuman effort is beyond me. I don't think that I can do it. Can anyone?

Either cave in and teach to the test, or rebel and raise hell and cause yourself a lot of trouble. Those who do the former are rewarded. Is it any wonder why they do? Take the easy road, and get rewarded. Take the high road and get scorned and humiliated. Is that what being an educator is all about, Ken? Isn't there any more than that to look forward to? Should I spend the next 30 years of my life in an uphill battle that I cannot win, when I have so many other opportunities? Is it worth the headaches? I don't think that I'm strong enough to fake it just so that I can stay around just to do a little bit of good. I am at the end of my rope. Franklin Roosevelt said that when you get to the end of your rope, tie a knot and hang on. Well, I am hanging by a very small knot, and I'm slipping. I wish I had better news for you.

Convince me to stay in education, Ken. Or tell me it's time to leave. I need some advice, and I don't know a single person whose advice I value more than yours. If you feel like telling me off for unloading this on you, go ahead. I probably deserve it. If you want to tell me to buck up and quit whining, do that. Or tell me that education needs people like me. Just tell me the truth.

Andy

Andy is a real person and this is a real letter. He is one of the graduate students I have worked with, and he has moved back to his mid-
western home state. He is an experienced high school and college math
teacher. He is a good teacher. What he says about his experience as an
educator in the present era of high-stakes testing and accountability is
compelling and chilling. It is an expression of both hope and despair.
And I don't think his story is at all unique.

In a way, this book is dedicated to Andy and all the good educators
like him who are struggling to do their best in an increasingly frustrating policy environment. And although critical, this book is intended to
be more about hope than despair. In this chapter, I offer a brief perspective on the problems and pitfalls of accountability, and then share some
important claims that I think can be defended and that constitute the foci
for subsequent chapters. In the final chapter, I return to critical analysis
but also to alternative perspectives that offer hope for more responsible
practices.

ACCOUNTABILITY AND ITS PROBLEMS

Teaching is tough under any circumstance, and there will always be
better and worse teachers and better and worse conditions and circumstances in which to be teaching. It is unfortunate, indeed, as in Andy's
case, when a tough job is made even tougher by a policy context seem-
ingly more bent on threat and punishment than on encouragement and
real support for educational improvement. Although certainly debat-
able, it is my belief that this pretty much characterizes the current and
past contexts of high-stakes accountability as we begin the new millen-
nium.

Evidence continues to mount about teacher and principal demoralization and attrition over frustration about the effects of mandated testing for high-stakes accountability (Goodnough, 2001; Jones, Jones,
Hardin, Chapman, Yarbrough, & Davis, 1999; McNeil, 2000; Whitford &
Jones, 2000; Winerip, 2003). Some are getting angry enough to become
activists in boycotting tests and even in releasing test items (e.g.,
"Chicago Teachers," 2002; Gehring, 2002). Some are resorting to cheating
(e.g., Hoff, 2000; Keller, 2002; Sandham, 1999). And, tragically, there may
be even more horrible outcomes.[1]

Negative reactions are not limited just to educators. All across the
nation, students and parents have gotten into the fray (Manzo, 2001;
Schrag, 2000). The recent Phi Delta Kappan/Gallup poll (Rose & Gallup,

2003) clearly indicates the skepticism of parents toward standardized tests and their utility in judging their children and their children's schools for high-stakes accountability. And legal challenges have begun or are underway in several states to counter the fallout from high-stakes testing and accountability practices. Notwithstanding the U.S. Supreme Court's reluctance thus far to consider cases against high-stakes exit examinations, for example, the Louisiana case (Walsh, 2002), momentum against the use of tests as gatekeepers is mounting and may eventually lead to a successful challenge. Allowing the use of basic-skills (or minimum competency) tests as gatekeepers (e.g., for high school graduation) is one thing; but when substantial numbers of middle- and upper-class students start failing high-standards exit exams, the protests and legal challenges are likely to pick up a real head of steam.

No wonder some states are already backing off and even contemplating how to make it easier to pass their mandated tests (Bowman, 2001; Dillon, 2003; Schemo, 2002). But the real injustice, ironically, is to the very students high-stakes accountability advocates claim to be concerned most about—economically poor students and students of color (Orfield & Kornhaber, 2001). These students are clearly the victims of the fallout of high-stakes accountability practices in disproportionately higher numbers (Jacob, 2001).

And what is the fallout? Consider the less-than-encouraging studies of the "Texas miracle" and the long-term efforts in Kentucky. According to the extensive analysis of the available data by Haney (2000), "Texas schools are devoting a huge amount of time and energy to preparing students specifically for TAAS [Texas Assessment of Academic Skills]...Emphasis on TAAS is hurting more than helping teaching and learning...Emphasis on TAAS is particularly harmful to at-risk students ... Emphasis on TAAS contributes to retention in grade and dropping out of school" (sect. 8, p. 6). The analysis by McNeil (2000) essentially reports very similar findings and conclusions.

The story in Kentucky is also similar. According to Whitford and Jones (2000), "Kentucky's accountability approach has undermined the very changes in teaching and learning that it was intended to promote, calling into question the use of performance assessment for high-stakes accountability" (p. 21).

Sadly, all this fallout is predictable and has been well-known long before the current incarnation of high-stakes accountability. We've had lots of experience in this country over the past several decades and more of test-driven accountability schemes designed to hold educators' and students' feet to fire. A good summary of the problems and pitfalls is provided by Heubert and Hauser (1999). Specific issues are addressed by Shepard (1991) on the effects of high-stakes testing on classroom instruction, by Shepard and Smith (1989) on the effects of flunking students in their formative development as learners, and by Nolen, Haladyna, and Hass (1992) on troubling issues more generally with achievement tests. Buly and Valencia (2002) have noted recently the particularly pernicious effects of unwarranted and oversimplistic assumptions about the meaning of setting performance standards on high-stakes, on-demand tests. In their comprehensive analysis of the patterns of failure for those kids "below the bar," they conclude:

> No single measure or intervention can possible meet the needs of all, or even most, of the students who are experiencing reading difficulty....We must remember that "below the bar" are individual children with different needs, and behind them are teachers who need policies that support thoughtful teaching and learning. (p. 235)

And once again, the children and youth who are really hurt most by all this continue to be those in poorer communities and in grossly under-funded and poorly staffed schools (Kozol, 1991; Payne & Biddle, 1999). Ironically, and sadly, the trend toward "takeovers" of "failing schools" not only appears to be ill-conceived but may end up hurting even more the very students these measures are presumably designed to protect (Malen, Croninger, Muncey, & Redmond-Jones, 2002). There is no way, I would suggest, that reasonable arguments can be made that students in such systems have equal opportunities to learn. And it may well be that this kind of argument will ultimately win the day in court; see, for example, the case of *Williams et al. v. State of California* (American Civil Liberties Union, 2001; Chapter 5, this volume).

Perhaps the saddest part of all is that there is really no solid evidence that these kinds of heavy-handed, test-based, accountability policies really work in meaningful and enduring ways. First of all, if they did, we would have improved public education long ago or at least stopped hearing about how bad our schools are. Simple logic suggests that given all the efforts since the early 1970s with minimum competency approaches, coupled with more recent efforts ostensibly focused on world class standards, we would have heard about substantial improvements by now.[2]

The counter argument, of course, is that even with this history of testing and accountability, there has never been a real emphasis on hooking rewards and sanctions to student test scores such as in the current high-stakes environment. But what do we know from this environment over the past half decade or more? It still doesn't seem to be working in any substantial or consistent way, and, even based on analyses by high-stakes accountability advocates, is unlikely to ever work in satisfactory and tidy ways (Brady, 2003; Finn, 2002).

Emerging nearly every month are new studies documenting the failure of high-stakes testing and accountability strategies and their predictable fallout (e.g., Casas, 2003; Cimbricz, 2002; Gándara, Rumberger, Maxwell-Jolly, & Callahan, 2003; Grant, 2002; Livingston & Livingston, 2002; Mathison & Freeman, 2003; Mintrop, 2002; Rigsby & DeMulder, 2003). Yet there are some studies still trying to find the pony in the manure pile. At best, the results from these studies are mixed. For example, reporting on the June 2002 conference "Taking Account of Accountability: Assessing Politics and Policy" held at the Kennedy School of Government (Harvard University), Olsen (2002) notes the teeter-totter nature of claims, even of interpretations by competent policy analysts of data on the same long-term reform initiatives (e.g., Chicago public schools).

Other competent policy analysts who have spent considerable time studying the difficulties of major, standards-based, high-stakes accountability initiatives (e.g., Elmore & Burney, 1997) know how simplistic and wrong-headed a test-driven accountability model can be. Commenting on the No Child Left Behind Act of 2001, for example, Elmore (2002) notes:

> This is an "accountability bill" that utterly fails to understand the institutional realities of accountability in states, districts, and schools.... In the history of federal education policy, the disconnect between policy and practice has never been so evident, nor so dangerous. Ironically, the conservative Republicans who control the White House and the House of Representatives are sponsoring the single largest—and most damaging—expansion of federal power over the nation's education system. (p. 1)

My guess is that the empirical case for the effectiveness of current high-stakes accountability will suffer the same fate as research, for example, on Head Start, class size, and whether money matters in public education. Depending upon ideological alliances, the same data or similar data will be used to draw opposite conclusions. Currently, this is illustrated well by the work of Amrein and Berliner (2002), on the one hand, and that of Raymond and Hanushek (2003) on the other.

Sadly, whether pro or con, these sorts of warring, empirical studies are all based solely on point-in-time, on-demand test scores, and pretty small, incremental, average gains or losses at that. Does anyone seriously believe that what a kid scores on an on-demand test really represents anything more than a small sample of highly contextualized paper-and-pencil behavior, ostensibly having something to do with teaching and learning, and, these days, a lot to do with a heavy dose of test preparation? Surely, what matters more is the cumulative impact of teaching and learning and the future potentials of each child and young adult in the care of our public schools. A test score is a mighty poor indicator of a human being's potential to become all that he or she can be (Scheffler, 1985). (I will have more to say about this in my concluding chapter.)

In my view, therefore, debates about whether or not high-stakes testing and accountability "works" cannot be resolved by looking at outcomes based on high-stakes tests! The issues "at stake" are far deeper than that, and arguments based on test scores diminish considerably serious moral and pedagogical concerns. Independent of their analysis of test score results, for example, Amrein and Berliner (2002) propose an interesting social sciences version of the Heisenberg Uncertainty Principle: "The more important that any quantitative social indicator becomes in social decision-making, the more likely it will be to distort and corrupt the social process it is intended to monitor" (p. 5). And as they report in their study, as has been reported in so many others, there is much support for this hypothesis:

> Because there are numerous reports of unintended consequences associated with high-stakes testing policies (increased drop-out rates, teachers' and schools' cheating on exams, teachers' defection from the profession, all predicted by the uncertainty principle), it is concluded that there is need for debate and transformation of current high-stakes testing policies. (p. 2)

Although it seems like a never-ending job description, educators must continue to hold the "accountabilists" accountable for their rationales and actions, and that is the primary purpose of this book. I first ran across the neologisms "accountablism" and "accountabilist" in a wonderful little critique of accountability, 1970s style, by Martin, Overholt, and Urban (1976). I think these are still useful terms to signal an alluringly simplistic ideology that has captured the attention of many, both right and left, on the political spectrum. And notwithstanding claims today of new-found accountability concepts and practices, Martin, Overholt, and Urban's rendition of the ideology in the 1970s is remarkably contemporary:

> The notion that all or most educational objectives should be couched in behavioral terms, the requirement that pedagogy be competence- or per-

formance-based, the insistence on a strategy of education evaluation which limits itself to that which can be observed and measured, and a call for the use of techniques of behavioral control which depend on an assumed instrumental relationship between means ... and ends. (p. 3)

Today, for example, if you go to the Fordham Foundation web site (www.edexcellence.net) and click on "standards, tests, and accountability," you'll find great optimism about what is essentially an old paradigm: "For too long, U.S. education has lacked meaningful standards and avoided real accountability. Thankfully, this is starting to change. The quest for educational accountability relies on a three-legged stool: standards, assessment, and consequences." In effect, whether we talk objectives or standards, minimum competency or world-class, the core ideology continues to hold promise for test-driven changes in teaching and learning, and rewards or punishments (high-stakes) to alter behaviors of educators and their students who apparently wouldn't do so otherwise.

Remarkably absent in this rationale is the need for ongoing professional development so prevalent (and costly) in the corporate world. And remarkably implicit is the pernicious assumption that many schools, educators, and children can make great changes unfettered by the inequitable and often miserable conditions and circumstances within which they exist, try to teach, and try to learn.

None of us who have contributed to this book are against standards. None of us believe that there are no good uses for test-based assessment or evaluation strategies. All of us believe that appraisal is important, that the public has a right to know how well schools are educating their children, and that the very nature of education itself should model good inquiry and reflective practice. All of us, however, are deeply concerned about what happens when heavy-handed accountability schemes get superimposed on the complexities of schooling practice.

In setting forward their "95 theses" on reforming evaluation practice, Lee Cronbach and his colleagues (1981) were well aware of the important distinctions between evaluation as educative and accountability as manipulative:

Accountability emphasizes looking back in order to assign praise or blame; evaluation is better used to understand events and processes for the sake of guiding future activities.

A demand for accountability is a sign of pathology in the political system. (p. 4)

Rooting out this pathology and developing more responsible practices require using what we already know about good teaching, learning, and assessment, and about the conditions and circumstances within which good educational practices can flourish, and drawing on centuries of experience with accountability of one form or another in public education.

In constructing this book, therefore, I first put forward a series of eight claims for more responsible accountability and a short paragraph describing each. I then asked contributing authors to unpack these claims (Chapters 1-8, this volume). Then I received their papers, and, in several cases, modified my initial claims and descriptive paragraphs. One of my goals was to get clearer about some of the complex and contentious issues in high-stakes accountability arguments, and the contributors to this book helped me to do just that. Here, then, are the claims and the authors.

CRITICAL CLAIMS

Responsible accountability systems must pay attention to lessons of the past. This is an overarching claim that in many ways frames all of the chapters of this book. Specifically, though, the first two claims I will make target the contributions of two historians of education, and six more claims are unpacked by the six additional contributors to this book.

First, *responsible accountability systems must pay attention to the history of accountability paradigms and critical analyses of their successes and failures.* To what extent has accountability always characterized public education in one way or another, and have any of these efforts ever really been successful? I have suggested above that if accountability efforts had ever been successful in any substantial and sustained way, we should by now have established a mantra in this nation about how good schools have become instead of quite the opposite. What is needed, however, is a more nuanced and historical look at how accountability has been construed in the history of public education, and that is what Larry Cuban sets out to do in Chapter 1. Indeed, Cuban extracts interpretations from his historical analysis that problematizes, in instructive ways, the notion of whether or not accountability has "worked."

Second, *responsible accountability systems must pay attention to the history of schooling and attempts to change and standardize behavior through impositions of consequences.* Why is it so ingrained in Western thought that the only way to guarantee people will do well is to threaten them with dire consequences for doing worse? The basic rationale for high-stakes assessments and accountability — high school graduation tests, for example — is that without them, teachers and students will not take better teaching and learning seriously. Without the threat of punitive consequences, it is argued, people have no incentive to do better. But, as Nancy Beadie shows us in Chapter 2, these coercive notions have a long and troubling history in this nation, and there are both moral and strategic lessons to be learned.

Third, *responsible accountability systems must be clear that standards and assessment are not arbitrary and are subservient to reasoned judgment about the educational aims and ideals of schooling.* Perhaps present-day assessment and high-stakes accountability systems live up to this claim. But if they do, then, by inference, the aims and ideals of schooling in America must be a watery broth of numeracy and literacy soup. Nothing resembling educationally rich visions of critically minded human beings, human beings fully capable of continued learning and intellectual growth, is suggested by narrowly defined, on-demand tests and, more important, by the equally narrow pedagogical practices focused on passing such tests. How might a reasoned argument be framed about what matters, and what ought to matter, when it comes to fully educated human beings? In Chapter 3, Harvey Siegel constructs just such an argument and shows (via one case study) how present-day assessment and accountability systems fail in light of his argument.

Fourth, *responsible accountability systems must be sensitive to the complexity of the social, political, and economic circumstances within which this nation expects its public schools to function.* The inequities that continue to mark our most troubled schools demonstrate that racism and classism are still alive and functioning in our social fabric and, thus, in today's (and likely tomorrow's) schools. Ironically, the rhetoric of "closing the achievement gap," has been picked up by both the conservative right, who may be more interested in privatizing public schools by showing continued failure to close the "gap" and by the liberal left, who believe that high-stakes testing and accountability is the only way to keep demonstrating the "gap" and, therefore, putting pressure on schools to do something about it. What truly needs closing is the "rhetorical gap," the gap between urging the closure of the "gap" and the commitment of the enormous resources it would take to ameliorate the pernicious outcomes of poverty, racism, and discrimination. Having said this, there is much room for schools to do far more than they have in dealing with these effects, even if the "rhetorical gap" is not closed. It is tricky business talking about this without being labeled negatively in some way by various proponents from either the left or the right. How can a convincing argument be constructed that both doesn't let schools off the hook (within reason) yet doesn't put the onus on them — use them as convenient scapegoats — to solve what are still the nation's problems to solve? In Chapter 4, Pedro Noguera continues this critique and offers compelling and concrete policy initiatives that would need to be implemented if policy makers were serious about really narrowing the achievement gap.

Fifth, *responsible accountability systems must be as focused on schooling conditions and equitable opportunities for student learning as on what students should be learning.* Given the documented disparities in quality of education due to structural features like tracking within schools and the "savage inequalities" characterizing many of our inner city and urban (and some rural) schools, it is hard to defend the proposition that today's schools offer equal opportunities for student learning. This has legal as well as moral implications. It is morally indefensible for public schooling in a social and political democracy to stand by with full knowledge that significant numbers of children (usually poor and of color) are disenfranchised from a quality of education being received by wealthier (and usually White) students — not only in nearby districts or in the same state or even out of state but sometimes even in the same school district or, worse yet, the same school! It may well be the case that a definitive case will need to be won in the courts before any headway on authentic equity and opportunities for learning can be accounted for in our public schools. Jeannie Oakes, Gary Blasi, and John Rogers have firsthand experiences with just such a challenge, and in Chapter 5 they share with us the substantive arguments and prospects for legal (if not moral) resolution.

Sixth, *responsible accountability systems must attend to all the core purposes of public schooling in a political and social democracy.* If "what gets tested is what's taught" is the central rationale of high-stakes assessment and accountability systems, then it is astonishing and appalling that civic education is virtually absent from these systems. If teaching students their moral and intellectual responsibilities as critical and informed citizens in a democracy is a central purpose of public schooling, than surely we would have a responsible system of assessment based on civic education in all of its complexity. But we don't, and in Chapter 6, Roger Soder takes up the question "Why not?" Other critical areas could have been the focus of the larger issue here, for example, the arts (music, drama, pictorial art, etc.). Given the centrality, however, of civic education to sustaining a dynamic system of governance in a democracy (e.g., Barber, 1993), it seemed appropriate to use this domain of education in investigating the logic of accountability and the ideological issues that cut to its core.

Seventh, *responsible accountability systems for educational practices must themselves be guided by sound educational practices.* Although there is still much to be learned, much is already known about best educational concepts and practices and the reciprocal connections between teaching, learning, and assessment. Unfortunately, both the theory and practice of traditional, on-demand, high-stakes testing and accountability systems are at odds with a great deal known about good teaching, learning, and assessment. High-stakes testing/accountability schemes result in well-known, negative fallout (e.g., teacher demoralization and student dropout, particularly economically poor students and students of color) and counterproductive educational practices (e.g., narrowing of the taught curriculum by teaching to the test, student retention in grades, and turning away from good pedagogical practices like individualization and cooperative learning). Essentially, test-driven reform models require belief in the assumptions that (1) all children are ready to be assessed at the same time in the same way on the same things, (2) useful information of various types is not already available to teachers for making good instructional decisions about individual students, and, most astonishingly, (3) education should be driven by assessment rather than the other way around. To think alternatively, as Linda Mabry shows us in Chapter 7, requires debunking "test-driven improvement" rationales, arguing for the importance of professional judgment by educators and for active involvement of students in their own evaluations, and advocating sound, "educationally driven" pedagogical practices including individualization and accumulating and using relevant information on each student over the course of their K–12 educational experiences.

Finally, *responsible accountability systems must be as focused on the continued learning of educators as they are on that for students.* The paltry amount of resources directed at the professional development for teachers and administrators in the nation's schools is disgraceful. No major cutting-edge company today could maintain its edge in the marketplace if it spent less than 5% of its resources (about what most school districts have available) on professional development, yet educators are now called upon to teach to higher and higher standards with precious little in the way of in-service training. In Chapter 8, Pat Wasley addresses these big questions: What do we know about the impact of good teaching on the quality of schooling? What are the characteristics of the kind of professional development and learning community that can make a

difference in both the quality of educators' work lives and in all the valued outcomes for students?

Understanding and internalizing the implications of these claims, I
believe, are crucial to once and for all giving up an accountability paradigm has never served well the children of our nation. And until we give
it up, we are not likely to get on with real progress toward more responsible ways to appraise the education of our children and the success of
our public schools. So let's see how each author has helped us to further
understand these eight claims.

NOTES

1. Although the evidence is circumstantial, a strong case has been made that
principal Betty Robinson's suicide may well have been linked to the accounta-
bility-based threat she perceived of her school's closure and/or being fired from
her position. See "Was Betty Robinson" (n.d.) and the compelling letter written
by her curriculum director colleague Kate Kirby (2002).

2. I hasten to add that, contrary to what I believe is politically motivated
hype, I don't think public schooling is all that bad, generally, or that it has gotten worse over all these years. See, for example, the analyses of Bracey (2002) and
Berliner and Biddle (1995). However, the plight of economically poor students
and students of color in our public schools, particularly in our urban areas, is still
a disgrace by any standard.

REFERENCES

American Civil Liberties Union. (2001). Court allows CA schools lawsuit to pro-
    ceed as a class action, making case largest education lawsuit. Retrieved
    January 23, 2003, from http://www.aclu.org/StudentsRights/Students
    Rights.cfm?ID=9161&c=31
Amrein, A.L., & Berliner, D.C. (2002). High-stakes testing, uncertainty, and stu-
    dent learning. *Education Policy Analysis Archives, 10(18)*. Retrieved March 28,
    2002, from http://epaa.asu.edu/epaa/v10n18
Barber, B.R. (1993, November). America skips school. *Harper's*, 39–46.
Berliner, D.C., & Biddle, B.J. (1995). *The manufactured crisis: Myths, fraud, and the
    attack on America's public schools.* New York: Longman.
Bowman, D.H. (2001, September 5). Delayed again: Ariz. moves high school exit
    exam to 2006. *Education Week, 21(1)*, 27.
Bracey, G.W. (2002). *The war against America's public schools: Privatizing schools,
    commercializing education.* Boston: Allyn & Bacon.
Brady, R.C. (2003). *Can failing schools be fixed?* Washington, DC: Thomas B.
    Fordham Foundation.

Buly, M.R., & Valencia, S.W. (2002). Below the bar: Profiles of students who fail state reading assessments. *Educational Evaluation and Policy Analysis, 24*(3), 219–239.

Casas, M. (2003). The use of standardized tests in assessing authentic learning — A contradiction indeed. *Teachers College Record,* http://www.tcrecord.org. ID Number: 11211. Retrieved October 15, 2003.

Chicago teachers boycott CASE. (2002, Fall). *FairTest Examiner, 16*(4), 5.

Cimbricz, S. (2002). State-mandated testing and teachers' beliefs and practice. *Education Policy Analysis Archives, 10*(2). Retrieved January 10, 2002 from http://epaa.asu.edu/epaa/v10n2.html

Cronbach, L.J. & Associates. (1981). *Toward reform of program evaluation.* San Francisco: Jossey-Bass.

Dillon, S. (2003, May 22). States are relaxing education standards to avoid sanctions from federal law. *The New York Times,* p. A25.

Elmore, R.F. (2002). Testing trap. *Harvard Magazine, 105*(1). Retrieved January 21, 2003, from http://www.harvard-magazine.com/on-line/0902140.html

Elmore, R.F., & Burney, D. (1998, May). The challenge of school variability: Improving instruction in New York City's Community district #2. *CPRE Policy Bulletin.*

Finn, C.E. (2002). Making school reform work. *The Public Interest, 148,* 85–95.

Gandara, P., Rumberger, R., Maxwell-Jolly, J., & Callahan, R. (2003). English learners in California schools: Unequal resources, unequal outcomes. *Education Policy Analysis Archives, 11*(36). Retrieved October 9, 2003 from http://epaa.asu.edu/epaa/v11n36/.

Gehring, J. (2002, May 8). Vote to award diplomas defies state testing policy. *Education Week, 21*(34), 3.

Goodnough, A. (2001, June 14). Strain of fourth-grade tests drives off veteran teachers. *The New York Times,* p. A-1

Grant, S.G. (2002). An uncertain lever: Exploring the influence of state-level testing in New York State on teaching social studies. *Teachers College Record, 103*(3), 398–426.

Haney, W. (2000). *The myth of the Texas miracle in education. Education Policy Analysis Archives, 8*(41). Retrieved December 4, 2001, from http://epaa.asu.edu/epaa/v8n41/

Heubert, J.P., & Hauser, R.M. (Eds.). (1999). *High stakes: Testing for tracking, promotion, and graduation.* Washington, DC: National Academy Press.

Hoff, D.J. (2000, December 15). N.Y.C. probe levels test-cheating charges. *Education Week, 19*(16), 3.

Jacob, B. A. (2001). Getting tough? The impact of high school graduation exams. *Educational Evaluation and Policy Analysis, 23*(2), 99–121.

Jones, M.G., Jones, B.D., Hardin, B., Chapman, T.Y., Yarbrough, T., & Davis, M. (1999). The impact of high-stakes testing on teachers and students in North Carolina. *Phi Delta Kappan, 81*(3), 199–203.

Keller, B. (2002, January 16). Austin cheating scandal ends in no-contest plea, fine. *Education Week, 21*(18), 3.

Kirby, K. (2002, May 5). Principal who died was gifted, devoted educator. *The Atlanta Journal and Constitution*, p. JJ7.

Kozol, J. (1991). *Savage inequalities: Children in America's schools.* New York: Crown.

Livingston, D.R., & Livingston, S.M. (2002). Failing Georgia: The case against the ban on social promotion. *Education Policy Analysis Archives, 10*(49). Retrieved December 10, 2002 from http://epaa.asu.edu/epaa/v10n49/.

Malen, B., Croninger, R., Muncey, D., & Redmond-Jones, D. (2002). Reconstituting schools: "Testing" the "theory of action." *Educational Evaluation and Policy Analysis, 24*(2), 113–132.

Manzo, K. (2001, May 16). Protests over state testing widespread. *Education Week, 20*(36), 1, 26.

Martin, D.T., Overholt, G.E., & Urban, W.J. *Accountability in American education: A critique.* Princeton, NJ: Princeton Book Company.

Mathison, S., & Freeman, M. (2003). Constraining elementary teachers' work: Dilemmas and paradoxes created by state mandated testing. *Education Policy Analysis Archives, 11*(34). Retrieved September 25, 2003, from http://epaa.asu.edu/epaa/v11n34/

McNeil, L.M. (2000). *Contradictions of school reform: Educational costs of standardized testing.* New York: Routledge.

Mintrop, H. (2002). The limits of sanctions in low-performing schools: A study of Maryland and Kentucky schools on probation. *Education Policy Analysis Archives, 11*(3). Retrieved January 16, 2003 from http://epaa.asu.edu/epaa/v10n49/

Nolen, S.B., Haladyna, T.M., & Hass, N.S. (1992) Uses and abuses of achievement test scores. *Educational Measurement: Theory and Practice, 11*(2), 9–15.

Olsen, L. (2002, June 19). Accountability studies find mixed impact on achievement. *Education Week, 21*(41), 13.

Orfield, G., & Kornhaber, M.L. (Eds.). (2001). *Raising standards or raising barriers? Inequality and high-stakes testing in public education.* New York: The Century Foundation Press.

Payne, K.J., & Biddle, B.J. (1999). Poor school funding, child poverty, and mathematics achievement. *Educational Researcher, 28*(6), 4-13.

Rawls, J. (1971). *A theory of justice.* Cambridge, MA: Belknap/Harvard University Press.

Raymond, M.E., & Hanushek, E.A. (2003, Summer). High-stakes research. *Education Next,* 48-55.

Rigsby, L.C., & DeMulder, E.K. (2003). Teachers' voices interpreting standards: Compromising teachers autonomy or raising expectations and performances? *Education Policy Analysis Archives, 11*(44). Retrieved November 18, 2003, from http://epaa.asu.edu/epaa/v11n44/

Rose, L.C., & Gallup, A.M. (2003). The 35th annual Phi Delta Kappa/Gallup poll of the public's attitudes toward the public schools. *Phi Delta Kappan, 85*(2), 41–52.

Sandham, J.L. (1999, April 7). Exam-testing breaches put focus on security. *Education Week, 18*(30), 20, 23.

Schemo, D. J. (2002, October 15). Sidestepping of new school standards is seen. *New York Times*, A21.

Scheffler, I. (1985). *Of human potential.* Boston: Routledge & Kegan Paul.

Schrag, P. (2000, August). High stakes are for tomatoes. *The Atlantic Monthly*, 19–21.

Shepard, L.A. (1991.). *The effects of high-stakes testing on instruction.* Paper presented at the annual meeting of the American Educational Research Association, Chicago, IL

Shepard, L.A., & Smith, M.L. (Eds.) (1989). *Flunking grades: Research and policies on retention.* London: Falmer Press.

Sirotnik, K.A. (2002). Promoting responsible accountability in schools and education. *Phi Delta Kappan, 83*(9), 662–673.

The Gwinnett Citizen. (n.d.). *Was Betty Robinson trying to tell us something?* Retrieved January 16, 2003 from http://gwinnettcitizen.com/Editorial/bettyrobinson.html

Walsh, M. (2002, March 6). Court declines case challenging promotion-assessment ties. *Education Week, 21*(25), 30.

Whitford, B.L., & Jones, K. (Eds.). (2000). *Accountability, assessment, and teacher commitment: Lessons from Kentucky's reform efforts.* Albany: State University of New York Press.

Winerip, M. (2003, May 28). The changes unwelcome, a model teacher moves on. *The New York Times.* Retrieved May 28, 2003, from http:www.nytimes.com/2003/05/28/education

CHAPTER 1

Looking Through the Rearview Mirror at School Accountability

Larry Cuban

- State Tests Are Becoming a Graduation Hurdle: Eighteen states ... deny diplomas to seniors who fail state tests (Mathews, 2001)
- Some Educators Win $25,000 Bonus as Test Scores Rise (Kollars, 2001)
- Pennsylvania Targets 11 Districts for Takeover (Johnston, 2000)

These headlines illustrate the individual and collective consequences built into present accountability structures that touch the daily lives of millions of students, hundreds of thousands of teachers, and tens of thousands of administrators in U.S. public schools. Neither the first nor last time that policy makers have installed accountability measures into schools, appraising previous efforts at fixing responsibility for the quality of schooling may illuminate the present moment. Car drivers habitually look through the rearview mirror to negotiate traffic safely; perhaps a pause to look into the past to grasp why accountability structures with personal and collective consequences are so pervasive now may render valuable insights and inform future policy making.

Holding Accountability Accountable. ISBN 0-8077-4464-6 (paper), ISBN 0-8077-4465-4 (cloth). Prior to photocopying items for classroom use, please contact the Copyright Clearance Center, Customer Service, 222 Rosewood Drive, Danvers, MA, 01923, USA, telephone (978) 750-8400.

EARLY EFFORTS AT MAKING PUBLIC SCHOOLS ACCOUNTABLE

At no time in the history of U.S. public schools have those responsible for schools been unaccountable. Assuredly, the aims of accountability, its means, who is answerable to whom and for what actions have shifted over time, but responsibility has been fixed and durable for nearly two centuries. Let me unpack this claim.

With the early 19th-century stirrings of tax-supported public education, the state-chartered district school board with elected trustees was legally obligated to the local community to ensure that children who attended public school were adequately housed, taught, and had materials to achieve the community's goals for its public schools. Annual elections of school board members determined to what degree voters were satisfied with their schools. In rural districts with one-room schoolhouses, which characterized most U.S. public schools until the end of the 19th century, this rudimentary form of accountability sufficed.

With the emergence of an industrial economy in New England and the rapid growth of cities, schools multiplied. Boards of education found it hard to supervise ever-increasing numbers of schools, examine teachers and students, and ensure that school funds were spent efficiently. To manage more schools and oversee students, for example, Boston's elected school committee had 7,000 students in 19 schools. They adopted "in addition to the usual mode of oral examination, the plan of submitting . . . a series of printed questions on all subjects studied" (Wigdor & Garner, 1982, p. 179).

An efficiency measure, the test of 30 questions was given to half of the eighth grade and revealed many students failing one or more subjects. The School Committee published the results. Over time, such short-answer tests became standardized for each subject and spread to many cities, becoming the basis for high school entrance exams. Although in these decades few students continued their education beyond grammar school, these entrance exams made it possible for district administrators to compare the performance of eighth-grade students who took the high school exam and then exert control over curriculum, teachers, and time schedules.

By the end of the Civil War, most city school boards had appointed a superintendent to carry out administrative duties. Now, the chain of command to determine efficient use of tax funds stretched from the school board to the superintendent to individual principals in schools across the city and, finally, to teachers in separate classrooms within each school. Achievement tests helped school boards and superintendents assess what teachers taught and what students learned in schools within their districts. Rarely, however, were these results made available to the public.

Eventually, interdistrict performance surfaced in the work of medical doctor Joseph Mayer Rice in 1897. He investigated two different districts, one that used 15 minutes per day to teach spelling at different grade levels and the other that used 30 minutes a day. He asked students in both districts to spell words from a common list. He found that the extra 15 minutes in one district made no significant difference in student results. Here, again, the results of these achievement tests were used to prod school administrators and teachers to use classroom time, the curriculum, and activities efficiently to improve their effectiveness (Graham, 1967). Although Rice was unsuccessful at first in getting districts to adopt standardized achievement tests to evaluate their curriculum and instruction, by World War I, at the urging of professional associations of teachers and superintendents, school boards across the nation were using more than 200 achievement tests in elementary and secondary schools — 11 in arithmetic alone (Resnick, 1980).

By the first decade of the 20th century, school boards and superintendents were also using achievement tests to determine why so many students left school at the age of 11 or 12. Both employers and school officials wanted students to stay in school beyond the fifth or sixth grade and even attend high school. The former sought more skilled workers to fill jobs in an increasingly industrialized economy and the latter wanted to make schooling at the upper grades available to more and more youth. Twelve-year-old school leavers represented a waste of scarce resources (Lazerson & Grubb, 1974; Resnick, 1980; Wigdor & Garner, 1982).[1]

Holding school boards and superintendents responsible for efficiently managing per-pupil costs in urban districts, however, went beyond voters electing school boards, the boards hiring superintendents, and using standardized achievement tests. Led by fervent business and civic-minded progressives in the early decades of the 20th century, who sought to bring order to an ever sprawling industrialized and urbanized America, reformers rolled up their sleeves and plunged into changing institution after institution, including the schools.

Many of these progressives believed that society had irrevocably changed. The traditional institutions of the family, church, and work that discharged core social responsibilities for instilling values, knowledge, and skills in the next generation, they claimed, could no longer be relied upon, particularly in cities. Urban slums were common. Poverty, immigrants' cultures, factories, and sweat shops splintered the family's traditional role in rearing their children. Schools, they said, had to pick up family responsibilities. And schools were made into custodial institutions. Children received medical and dental care, ate hot meals, learned to be American, and prepared to work in an industrialized economy. The school was expected to knit together what industrialization and urbanization had unraveled and, in doing so, make a better society (Cremin, 1961; Reese, 1986; Tyack, 1974).

Progressives also believed that abundant information drawn from scientific research and experts made available to the public could make government, business, religion, the justice system, and education more efficient and effective (Schudson, 1998). Lawyer Louis Brandeis put it best in 1913: "Publicity is justly commended as a remedy for social and industrial diseases. Sunlight is said to be the best disinfectant; electric light the best policeman" (Wynne, 1972, p. 193). More and better information would motivate, shame, and ultimately prod school boards and administrators into making schools efficient and lead to a more rational, democratic, and humane society.

In public education, civic-minded professors and a new breed of superintendents, sharing this belief in the transforming power of information, fueled the school survey movement before and after World War I. Large-scale surveys put experts into districts. They counted every public dollar and how it was spent on buildings, curriculum, supervision, teachers, methods of teaching, students, and school organization. According to one advocate, the main purpose of these surveys, was

> to educate the public ... to tell them in simple terms all the salient facts about their public schools and then to rely upon the common sense, the common insight, and the common purpose of the people as the first great resource in working out their problem. (Tyack & Hansot, 1982, p. 166)

Public reports of standardized achievement tests and school surveys in the closing decades of the 19th century and early decades of the 20th century were rational efforts to increase administrator and teacher efficiency in managing overcrowded schools, teaching classes of 50-plus students, and reducing the number of 12-year-old school leavers. But were they instruments of accountability?

The answer turns on defining accountability. If accountability means fixing responsibility — either moral or legal or both — and providing relevant information on the efficiency and effectiveness of schools to those who make informed decisions, then what I have described is clearly accountability. In these decades, elected rural and urban school boards were legally responsible to voters in their districts; boards hired and fired superintendents. They used the achievement tests of the day and school surveys to inform the public and compare the quality of their district against that of others. Then boards and superintendents rendered an account in annual reports of their goals, activities undertaken, and monies spent.

In the years before and after World War II, what mattered most to school boards, superintendents, academics, and the informed public was efficient use of limited resources in providing modern buildings with enough rooms and desks to house students, indoor plumbing, qualified teachers, and sufficient textbooks to educate all who entered school. Policy makers, practitioners, parents, and researchers viewed schools with these features as good schools.

After World War II, major social, economic, and political changes produced another, more dramatic, version of accountability that transformed the meaning of a quality schooling and which goals should be pursued.

MAKING SCHOOLS ACCOUNTABLE SINCE 1965

Between the U.S. Supreme Court's *Brown v. Board of Education* decision (1954) and the Watts civil disturbance in Los Angeles in 1965, civil rights and education dominated the domestic political agenda. The launch of a beach-ball–size satellite in 1957 demonstrated the Soviet Union's rocket capacity to develop intercontinental missiles. Foreign policy experts and pundits concluded that the Soviets were winning the Cold War arms race because of a superior system of schooling. In the wake of *Sputnik* orbiting the earth, President Dwight D. Eisenhower signed the National Defense Education Act in 1958. A cascade of reforms raised graduation requirements in math and science, added programs for the gifted, and introduced advanced placement (AP) high school courses to speed entry into colleges.

Simultaneously with schools' being drafted to fight the Cold War, a swelling civil rights movement scored victory after victory in the South. The election of Lyndon Johnson in the backwash of the Kennedy assassination produced unprecedented civil rights and education legislation and a managerial efficiency movement in government borrowed from the military and private sector. With a mighty shove from President

Lyndon B. Johnson, the U.S. Congress passed the Civil Rights Act (1964) and the Elementary and Secondary Education Act (ESEA) of 1965 that provided for the first time funds for poor schoolchildren to get a better education and improve their life chances. Senator Robert F. Kennedy (NY), fearful of districts' diverting and wasting federal funds, attached an amendment to Title I of ESEA that required annual evaluations. He wanted to "hold educators responsive to their constituencies and to make educational achievement the touchstone of success in judging ESEA" (McLaughlin, 1975, p. 3).

Johnson also ordered all federal executive departments to use business-inspired managerial techniques such as PPBS (planning, programming, budgeting systems), PERT (program evaluation and review technique), and MBO (managing by objectives), rational procedures first applied in the U.S. Department of Defense under its former Ford CEO, Robert McNamara. The convergence of these unlikely (and unpredictable) circumstances helps explain the dramatic shift in school accountability and definition of a quality education, from providing access to an adequate schooling and efficient use of resources for well over a century and a half—the earlier definition of a good school—to a heightened responsibility for student outcomes and a performance-based definition of high-quality education (Lessinger, 1970; Wise, 1978).

By the end of the 1960s, even after eye-popping legislation poured billions of dollars into districts with large percentages of poor children, critics from the political left and right claimed that schools were failing miserably. From the left, critics pointed to evaluations mandated under ESEA and independent assessments that racist organizational, curricular, and teaching practices were deeply embedded in largely White-staffed urban and rural public schools. They pointed to the reluctance of policy makers and school officials to desegregate urban schools and streamline their massive bureaucracies. Inaction by school boards and administrators meant that dropouts, youth unemployment, drug use, and crime would continue to plague minority communities (Kohl, 1968; Rogers, 1968; Schrag, 1967).

From the political right, angry critics pointed to the major increases in federal and state spending for both urban and suburban schools, and yet these very same schools had become infected with the late-1960s counterculture. They pointed to the growing reluctance of suburban school authorities to stamp out rising drug use and the capitulation of administrators to such fads as open-space schools and open (or neo-progressive) classrooms. Schools were failing to transmit societal core values to the next generation.

Even when a "back-to-basics" movement for more traditional elementary schools emerged, critics applauded but wanted far more rigor. Fewer high school students took 3 years of math, science, and foreign language. Steep declines in Scholastic Aptitude Test (SAT) scores worried both business and civic leaders because the best and the brightest were supposed to go on to college and become the scientists, managers, and CEOs of future firms (Brodinsky, 1977; Ravitch, 1983).

Employer criticism of high school graduates unprepared for the workplace, violence in urban schools, and the flight of White middle-class families from cities to suburbs after the late-1960s' racial disturbances in cities made it easy for faultfinders from the left and right to fix blame on American public schools as a source of larger national problems. Within this climate of opinion, business and civic leaders emerged with plans to make schools better and more productive. Business-inspired designs for a better education, they argued, would stimulate economic growth and worker productivity, reduce social instability, and enhance chances of individuals to become financially successful (Tyack & Cuban, 1995).

Building on the "back-to-basics" campaign in the early 1970s, business and civic leaders prodded legislatures to reform schools. By the end of the decade, two thirds of the states had mandated that high school students had to pass minimum competency tests to graduate to show the public how accountable educators were (Jaeger & Tittle, 1980).

By 1983, a presidential commission of corporate and public leaders and educators had reported their assessment of public schools in the *Nation at Risk*. This report crystallized the growing sense of unease with public schooling in the business community by tightly coupling mediocre student performance on national and international tests to mediocre economic performance in the global marketplace (Commission on Excellence in Education, 1983).

After the *Nation at Risk,* state after state increased high school graduation requirements, lengthened the school year, and added more tests for students to take. In 1989, President George Bush convened the 50 governors to discuss education. They called for six national goals (later expanded to eight), one of which asked American students to rank first on international tests in math and science by the year 2000. Throughout the 1990s, urged on by President Clinton and federal policy makers, state after state mandated curricular and performance standards, new tests, and holding principals, teachers, and students answerable for improving academic achievement.

The 2000 election of former Texas Governor George W. Bush, the first President of the United States to hold a master's degree in business administration, brought to the nation's attention a chief executive who had promoted school improvement in his state and was eager to apply lessons he had learned there to the rest of the country. Bush appointed Houston Superintendent Rod Paige—who carried a national reputation for working closely with the city's business community to raise minority students' test scores—as his U.S. Secretary of Education and rolled out legislation that touched every single public school student in the nation. Resolutely backed by national business associations and bipartisan to its core—Democratic Senator Ted Kennedy (MA) helped draft the bill and move it through the Senate—the No Child Left Behind (NCLB) Act elevated test-based accountability to federal policy for U.S. schools (Business Roundtable, 2002; NCLB, 2002).

The alliance of corporate leaders, public officials, and educators between the late-1970s and the present made the following assumptions:

- Future workforce would have far more minorities drawn from cities than the present one.
- Excessive school bureaucracy and a lack of accountability had lowered academic standards (particularly in math and science), undermined rigorous teaching, and graduated students, especially from urban schools, mismatched to the skill demands of an information-based workplace.
- Teachers and administrators knew how to improve teaching and learning and end the skills mismatch; professionals lacked the will, not expertise.
- Efficient management, high academic standards, increased competition among schools for students, and clear incentives and penalties would spur professionals to raise academic achievement.
- The best measure of improved teaching and learning was higher standardized test scores and that those scores would convert into better workplace performance (Kearns & Doyle, 1988; Marshall & Tucker, 1992; Reich, 1991; Thurow, 1992; Toch, 1991).

These assumptions led business and civic reform coalitions to press local, state, and federal policy makers for standards-based reform, more testing, and broader accountability structures in the 1990s. In a half-dozen cities, mayors fed up with local schools' poor performance took over control of their districts and publicly said that they were responsible for raising test scores. Currently, Maryland, Michigan, and Pennsylvania have stripped Baltimore, Detroit, and Philadelphia school boards of their authority and assumed control because of their persistent low performance (Cuban & Usdan, 2003; Kirst, 2002).

Forty-nine states have adopted standards of what their students should know and established tests to assess their performance. The number of states that administer student tests that are aligned with published standards in at least one subject climbed from 35 in 1998 to 41 in 2000. According to *Education Week* ("Quality Counts," 1999), 27 states rate schools primarily on the basis of test scores; and 14 states have authorized their departments of education to close and take over low-performing schools. In 18 states, students who fail the statewide graduation test do not receive diplomas. Ten more states have mandated that penalty to be enforced by 2008. In 13 states (as of 2000), cash payments or awards flow to schools that meet their targets and show continuous improvement. By 2001, all 50 states either produced or required local school boards to publish district or school report cards that included data on students' test performance, attendance, dropout and graduation rates, school discipline, student–teacher ratios, and financial information ("Quality Counts," 1999; "Quality Counts," 2000; Goertz & Duffy, 2001; Sanger, 2001; Wilgoren, 2000).

President Bush's NCLB Act takes the equity-rich slogan "All children can learn," borrowed from the basic premise of the Effective Schools movement in the late 1970s and early 1980s, and puts the full force of federal authority behind standards-based reform. The law requires all districts receiving federal funds to test every student in grades 3 through 8 in reading and mathematics and, by 2007, states must test students in science at least once in grades 3 through 5, 6 through 9, and 10 through 12. All districts are responsible for each group of students (i.e., test scores are disaggregated by ethnicity and race) to make "adequate yearly progress" toward being "proficient" in state standards. By 2014, every student must be "proficient." NCLB also mandates that those schools showing improvement will be rewarded and those that fail to meet targets for "adequate yearly progress" 2 years in a row will face "corrective action" and, ultimately, "restructuring." If a student is in a school identified as failing, the family could choose to send their child to another school at the district's expense (but not across district lines to another school system) (NCLB, 2002).

How costly has this explosion of testing and accountability since the 1970s been? Although the bill for additional state and local testing that will accumulate from NCLB has yet to be tallied, a rough approximation of the dollar costs of testing (purchased and locally designed), student information systems, and accountability report cards can be made. In the early 1990s, the General Accounting Office estimated that the average per-student test cost was $25. The estimate was for the actual per-student cost of the test ($15) and per-student average start-up development costs ($10) over a 3-year period (GAO, 1993). Drawing from federal and state sources, Carolyn Hoxby (2002) has compiled recent dollar costs of test-based accountability systems. For those states that have accountability systems in place in 2001, the highest spending state laid out $34 per student (or a third of a penny of its overall per-pupil expenditure); the lowest spending state, just under $2 (or two-hundredths of a cent).

As a percentage of total spending on public schools for the nation, no state spends *"even 1 percent* of its elementary and secondary school budget on accountability" (Hoxby, 2002, p. 69, emphasis in original). Policy makers would call this a splendid bargain—getting enormous bang for a fraction of a penny. The accountability-costs-too-much argument fails when one looks only at the dollars. There are, however, other less easily measured costs, such as the time teachers spend in class preparing for tests and the time that schools allocate for test preparation. Moreover, opportunity costs are seldom calculated for the curriculum teachers omit, school activities foregone, and experiences students miss in exchange for test preparation and actual time spent taking tests. Much anecdotal evidence from parents, teachers, teachers unions, and principals suggests that the costs for testing run far higher than estimates of dollars spent.[2]

If estimating costs of testing is far more complicated than actual dollars and cents, much less complex is estimating the sum total of nearly three decades of business involvement in schools through philanthropy, partnerships, and application of corporate practices. In these years, public schools have become more rational, efficient, and businesslike in governance, management, and organization. Certainly, since the mid-1970s, the purposes of accountability, the lines of responsibility, the means, and the outcomes have all become starkly transparent.

SUMMING UP AND PARTING THOUGHTS

Let me sum up the major points I have made in this chapter.

First, school boards have been accountable to voters and elected officials since the origins of tax-supported public schools.

Second, however, this constancy in generic accountability should not mask the major change that has occurred since 1965. A pre-1965 system of accountability was sharply focused on defining a good school as one that efficiently provided students access to adequate buildings, staff, and materials. Information from student testing and periodic surveys provided data to boards and administrators. Legally and morally, both answered to the public for maintaining this version of good schools. The post-1965 system of accountability, however, defined good schools as ones that have efficiently used their resources to yield improved students' academic achievement as measured by test scores. Accountability structures have relied largely on tests and reporting procedures that hold students, teachers, principals, superintendents, school boards, and mayors individually responsible for overall academic performance. This shift in what constitutes good schools and who is held responsible for achieving that type of school is, indeed, a sea change.

Third, external pressures for increased information- and test-based accountability attached to direct consequences for student outcomes have largely come from outside the schools. At the beginning of the 20th century, business-minded progressives committed to making the United States an orderly and economically competitive industrial nation saw more and better information as the solution for any problem, including the breakup of the traditional family, reduction in schools' inefficiencies, and inadequate worker preparation in schools. Toward the end of the same century, business and civic elites shared the same efficiency-minded impulse to have schools defend the nation against Soviet advances in the Cold War, eliminate poverty and racism, and prepare workers for a knowledge economy. Past and present reformers have aimed at making schooling (and other social and political institutions) more rational, efficient, and effective in solving local and national problems.

These points, however, miss answering a key question: Overall, has this remarkable, externally driven shift—in the meaning of quality schooling, the goals for schools, and accountability structures from pre-1965 to post-1965—improved schooling?

The key word in the question is *improved*. It is a word chock-full of values because it leaves the ultimate purpose of schooling unmentioned. "Improved" toward what end? Thus each reader's view of the purposes schools should serve is triggered by the verb. For me, also.

In answering this question and in the interest of full disclosure, I will no longer assemble data, establish the accuracy of evidence, and analyze multiple and incomplete sources. Although I will try hard to offer a balanced view, my values will surface in the remaining pages as I draw from my experiences as a teacher, superintendent, and historian of education for nearly five decades.

My answer is both yes and no. For the yes answer, four benefits, in my judgment, have flowed from the post-1965 standards-based testing and outcome-driven accountability structures. First, forming civic and business coalitions twice in one century to reform schools has brought together disparate constituencies in a community-wide effort to improve public schools, a core social institution. No easy task in modern times. Such evidence of civic capacity-building remains rare, usually reserved for securing sports franchises and stadiums. Any time such coalitions form and remain united around an institution for sustained periods of time, the entire community can benefit. The potential danger of such civic and business-led unity, however, is a narrowing of the broad goals sought for tax-supported public schools over the past two centuries, thus ill-serving the best interests of academically, culturally, and socially diverse children living in a democracy.

Second, the quest for equity of access to ensure equality of opportunity that marked reformers' efforts to promote educational growth in the 19th and 20th centuries has continued into the 21st century for those children who have been historically least well served: the poor, minorities, and newcomers to the United States. In pursuing the valued ideal of equity, however, there are clear dangers. Bipartisan and business-inspired reformers can reduce the historic goals of public schooling to preparing workers for a knowledge-based economy and then freeze-dry that goal into equalizing test scores between minority and White students. There is no question in my mind that the equity impulse is worthwhile and essential for a democratic society, but severe risks exist in placing that impulse into policy and then into classrooms.

Third, the dramatic shift from assessing the efficiency of what schools do with their resources to assessing outcomes from schooling is, on balance, beneficial. American can-do pragmatism and a business-driven passion for the storied "bottom line" gives long overdue attention to evaluating specific outcomes of schooling. Educators have seldom clamored to be first in line to assess whether desired outcomes have been achieved. Amid plenty of criticism of standardized and criterion-referenced tests, pressing for measurable outcomes, nonetheless, captures certain specific teaching and learning outcomes. How many students graduate, get jobs, and enter postsecondary institutions are useful indicators of schools' overall performance if the larger purpose is preparing students for jobs and college. So are measures of student, parent, and teacher satisfaction with their schools. As proxies for desired outcomes, these indicators point to the degree of success that educators have had in reaching certain goals.

Many educators and parents, on the other hand, have argued that serious purposes for schooling, such as civic engagement, creativity, appreciation for the arts, curiosity, a socially just community, and personal well being cannot be easily measured as can, say, monthly profits or how much U.S. history students have learned. The past three decades in which test-driven and consequence-heavy accountability has attained prominence proved those educators correct. Except for a few foundations and hardy researchers, limited resources and effort have been expended to construct measures or render judgments of these important goals.

Fourth, the essential linkage between building teachers' and principals' knowledge and skills in particular arenas to improve their work, and by extension student effects, has been forged in the minds of policy makers, practitioners, researchers, and informed parents. Capacity-building of practitioners' knowledge and skills is crucial to any improvement in academic achievement. The linkage, however, challenges one of the cardinal assumptions of reformers—namely, that the cause of students' poor academic performance is the lack of will on the part of practitioners, not expertise. This may well explain—along with the enormous cost of investing in teacher and principal growth—why only splintered and erratic efforts at expanding the knowledge and skills of practitioners have been made nationally.

Beyond these benefits, however, I also see clear losses accruing not only from the measures used but from the accountability structures borrowed from the business sector that seek to ensure better school-wide performance.

First, the historic goals of tax-supported public schools in a democracy (e.g., building thoughtful and wise citizens, developing individual character, reducing inequities) have been telescoped by state and federal policy makers into one overriding, measurable, and narrow goal: Prepare everyone to go to college and then enter a knowledge-based workplace.

Second, because of the current test-based accountability mechanisms driving standards-based reform toward the above purpose for public schooling, only one version of a good school has been reaffirmed—a college preparatory model that begins in preschool and extends through high school graduation. There is little patience or support for other versions of good public schools that have had a verifiable history of responding well to academic, social, and political differences among children and parents, such as progressive, community-based, democratic, social-justice-oriented, and varied combinations of all of these (Cuban, 2003).

Third, the theory driving the present test-based accountability structures assumes that teachers and principals have the know-how to improve academic performance but lack the will. Ditto for students. A well-informed public and a system of incentives and penalties, holders of the theory believe, will prod educators and students to get off their duffs, pull up their socks, and do the right thing. In short, students' poor academic performance is entirely a school-induced problem; the solution, then, is school-based.

Such a simplistic theory is hostile to rival and complex explanations (e.g., uncredentialed teachers, large class sizes, family background, unemployment, and community poverty) for academic failure and gaps in achievement between White and minority students. The individual and collective costs run high in having a sole-source theory that places full responsibility upon the public school for moving the bottom quartile upward.

A school-based theory diverts public attention from other explanations that call for substantial investments in educating urban and rural poor and minority children before they come to school, reducing class size, securing qualified and experienced teachers, instituting a full employment policy, and reducing rural and urban poverty. These factors, rather than relying solely on schools, have ample research bases for showing strong linkages to students' academic performance. Such investments, of course, carry big-ticket prices.

Finally, these testing and accountability structures squeeze out other forms of assessment used and strongly supported by many researchers and practitioners. Student assessment, for example, through writing, projects, portfolios, and exhibitions are imperfect to be sure (and because they are labor-intensive, costs run considerably higher than group testing), but they have promise for getting at traditional and nontraditional outcomes consistent with broader goals of schooling.

Also ignored are other forms of whole school assessment that do not rely solely on test-driven accountability, such as Practice-Based Inquiry or School Accountability for Learning and Teaching (SALT). Both lean heavily upon teams of veteran practitioners examining carefully and fully the strengths and weaknesses of a school staff's efforts at teaching and closing the achievement gap. Public reports are made that offer concrete alternatives for improvement (Rhode Island Department of Education, 1997; Wilson, 1996).

So my double-headed answer of yes and no to the question of whether this remarkable, externally driven shift in the meaning of quality schooling and accountability from pre-1965 to post-1965 has improved schooling ends up where I began. If readers are convinced that the assumptions behind test-driven and consequential accountability are accurate, then those readers will nod in agreement to my yes and object to my no; other readers who have questioned the assumptions driving current efforts at accountability will deny the yes answer and respond with a head-shaking no, even adding to my list. For those who are unsure and want to think further on the matter—my target audience—I have offered these parting thoughts in the hope that policy makers, practitioners, researchers, and informed parents, who consider one's definition of a good school and accountability important, can profit from a look backward in the rearview mirror.

NOTES

1. After World War I, mass aptitude testing, which had been used to place nearly 2 million U.S. Army recruits in different jobs, was swiftly adapted to schools. Administrators needed help in efficiently placing the growing number of students into different curricula designed to match students to their future trajectory in the economy and society within the newly invented comprehensive high school and the emerging junior high school (Resnick, 1980; Wigdor & Garner, 1982). Ability testing for placement in curricula in secondary schools was not used to hold teachers, students, or administrators responsible for results.

2. At Rancho Bernardo High School near San Diego, California, where most students score well on their SATs and plan on attending universities, parents have received waivers for their college-bound sons and daughters to not take the state tests. The absence of these high-scoring students from school-wide totals has lowered the high school in state rankings and lost cash for the school, not to mention raising anger among realtors and other parents who have bought into the district precisely for their children to attend the high school. See Daniel Golden (2002).

REFERENCES

Brodinsky, B. (1977, March). Back to the basics: The movement and its meaning. *Phi Delta Kappan, 57*, 522–527.

The Business Roundtable (2002). http://brt.org/toolkit/toolkit.html

Commission on Excellence in Education. (1983). *A nation at risk*. Washington, DC: Government Printing Office.

Cremin, L. (1961). *Transformation of the school*. New York: Vintage.

Cuban, L. (2003). *Why is it so hard to get good schools?* New York: Teachers College Press.

Cuban, L., & Usdan, M. (Eds.). (2003). *Powerful reforms with shallow roots.* New York: Teachers College Press.

General Accounting Office. (1993). *Student testing.* GAO/PEMD-93-8. Washington, DC: U.S. Government Printing Office.

Goertz, M., & Duffy, M. (2001, May). *Policy Briefs, RB-33. Assessment and accountability across the 50 states.* Philadelphia: Consortium for Policy Research in Education.

Golden, D. (2002, December 24). Student's dream, principal's dread: The test not taken. *Wall Street Journal,* pp. A1, A6.

Graham, P. (1967). *Progressive education: From arcady to academe.* New York: Teachers College Press.

Hoxby, C. (2002). The cost of accountability. In W. Evers & H. Walberg (Eds.), *School accountability* (pp. 47–74). Stanford, CA: Hoover Institution Press.

Jaeger, R., & Tittle, C. (1980). *Minimum competency achievement testing.* Berkeley, CA: McCutchan Publishing Corporation.

Johnston, R. (2000, May 17). Pa. targets 11 districts for takeover. *Education Week, 1,* 26.

Kearns, D., & Doyle, D. (1988). *Winning the brain race: A bold plan to make our schools competitive.* San Francisco, CA: Institute for Contemporary Studies Press.

Kirst, M. (2002). *Mayoral influence, new regimes, and public school governance. RR-049.* Philadelphia: Consortium for Policy Research in Education, University of Pennsylvania.

Kohl, H. (1968). *36 Children.* New York: New American Library.

Kollars, D. (2001, January 8). Some educators win $25,000 bonus as test scores rise. The Sacramento Bee, p. 1.

Lazerson, M., & Grubb, N. (Eds.). (1974). *American education and vocationalism: Documents in vocational education, 1870–1970.* New York: Teachers College Press.

Lessinger, L. (1970). *Every kid a winner.* New York: Simon and Schuster.

Marshall, R., & Tucker, M. (1992). *Thinking for a living: Education and the wealth of nations.* New York: Basic Books.

Mathews, J. (2001, January 30). State tests are becoming a graduation hurdle. *Washington Post,* 14.

McLaughlin, M. (1975). *Evaluation and reform.* Cambridge, MA: Ballinger.

No Child Left Behind Act of 2001. (2002). Available from http://www.NoChildLeftBehind.gov/

"Quality counts." *Education Week* (1999, January 11).

"Quality counts." *Education Week* (2000, January 13).

Ravitch, D. (1983). *Troubled crusade.* New York: Basic Books.

Reese, W. (1986). *Power and promise of school reform.* London: Routledge & Kegan Paul.

Reich, R. (1991). *The work of nations.* New York: Alfred Knopf.

Resnick, D. (1980). Minimum competency testing historically considered. In D. Berliner (Ed.), *Review of Research in Education,* vol. 8 (pp. 3–29). Washington, DC: American Educational Research Association.

Rhode Island Department of Education. (1997). *SALT: A blueprint for school accountability for learning and teaching.* Final report. Rhode Island: Author.

Rogers, D. (1968). *110 Livingston St.* New York: Random House.

Sanger,. D. (2001, January 24). Bush pushes ambitious education plan. *The New York Times,* pp. A1, A14.

Schrag, P. (1967). *Village school downtown: Boston schools, Boston politics.* Boston: Beacon Press.

Schudson, M. (1998). *The good citizen : a history of American civic life.* New York: Martin Kessler Books.

Thurow, L. (1992). *Head to head: The coming economic battle among Japan, Europe, and America.* New York: Morrow.

Toch, T. (1991). *In the name of excellence.* New York: Oxford University Press.

Tyack, D. (1974). *One best system.* Cambridge, MA: Harvard University Press.

Tyack, D., & Cuban, L. (1995). *Tinkering toward utopia.* Cambridge, MA: Harvard University Press.

Tyack, D., & Hansot, E. (1982). *Managers of virtue.* New York: Basic Books.

Wigdor, A., & Garner, W. (1982). *Ability testing: Uses, consequences, and controversies.* Washington, DC: National Academy Press.

Wilgoren, J. (2000, August 2). For 2000, the G.O.P. sees education in a new light. *The New York Times,* p. A15.

Wilson, T. (1996). *Reaching for a better standard.* New York: Teachers College Press.

Wise, A. (1978). *Legislated learning.* Berkeley: University of California Press.

Wynne, E. (1972). *The politics of school accountability.* Berkeley, CA: McCutchan.

CHAPTER 2

Moral Errors and Strategic Mistakes: Lessons From the History of Student Accountability

Nancy Beadie

First, some distinctions. What comes under the rubric of "accountability" in current education reform is multiple and complex. For starters, I would distinguish at least four main systems of accountability in public education. The first operates at the level of the individual student. It is the system of student promotion and attainment that is controlled through the high school diploma. The second is institutional. It operates through districts and schools and is largely controlled through school funding law. The third is professional. It operates at the level of teachers and other professional educators and is controlled through certification. Finally, the fourth system of accountability is political. It operates through superintendents, school boards, politicians, and their constituencies. It is formally controlled through elections, though of course there are other ways of exercising political influence.

This chapter focuses on the student component of these systems, specifically on the history of standardized achievement tests, the high school diploma, and other ways of systematizing student promotion and attainment. One of the main points of the chapter, however, is

connective. The aim is to highlight the moral and historical significance of current efforts to link student-based systems of accountability with other forms of accountability in education. In the previous
chapter, Larry Cuban looked at the issue of *school* accountability from
a historical perspective. He claimed that a significant historical shift
occurred in school accountability in the mid-1960s. Before 1965, school
accountability consisted of making responsible use of public
resources, that is, using those resources efficiently to provide the best
possible education for everyone. Since 1965, however, school accountability has changed. Influenced in part by business leaders, legislators
have moved toward tying school funding to student outcomes.
Systems of school accountability, in other words, are increasingly
being linked to systems of *student* accountability.

The general mood in current education reform is that this linkage is
good. Even though there is much debate about the terms of such a connection, there is general agreement that schools should be held responsible for how well they support student achievement. Compelling arguments are made that this linkage finally provides the political and
financial leverage necessary to make schools and teachers concentrate
effectively on meeting the needs of failing students. Another way of
looking at this historical shift, however, is that students are being made
an instrument of school accountability. The working idea is that if
enough students fail and fail with dramatic enough consequences,
schools will be forced to become more effective. To frame the issue in
this way is to begin to see some of the moral dimensions of this kind of
accountability. Failure, after all, has consequences for students as well as
schools. As we look back into the history of student accountability, the
moral significance of this fact appears more profound.

HISTORICAL ORIGINS OF STUDENT ACCOUNTABILITY

To use the phrase "student accountability" is already to perform a
metaphorical sleight of hand that imports a language of finance into
education. If we step back for a moment and think about education in
moral, psychological, social, intellectual, or cultural terms, we might
come up with a number of different metaphors for the educational
process. We might, for example, think about the idea of "initiation" into
a culture, or into adulthood. We might think about "apprenticeship" into
the standards and techniques of a craft or set of practices. We might
think about the "cultivation" or "growth" of a human organism or the

"formation" of a human self or soul. It's worth noting that none of these ways of conceiving of education leads in the direction of accounting. To get to the metaphor of accounting one has to think not about education but about schooling, and not just about schooling but about school systems. Conceptually speaking, in other words, the phrase "student accountability" has a lot more to do with the educational system than it does with education. It refers to the rationalization of criteria and procedures by which students are assigned to certain units of the system and moved from one unit of the system to another.

Moving from the conceptual to the historical, we can ask what the origins of this form of accounting were. What is loosely referred to here as "student accountability" is actually a set of systems that developed in the 19th century to address a set of historical problems. The first of these systems is now so fundamental to the organization and administration of schooling that we seldom recognize it as a historical innovation. This is the system of graded schooling, or the hierarchical organization of schools into separate classes or levels of instruction through which individual children are expected systematically to progress.

Graded schooling was a reform of the late 18th and early 19th centuries. It developed to address the problem of instructing masses of children at once, and in this sense was a product of the growing consensus that the state had an obligation to provide schooling for everyone. At its most extreme, graded schooling involved the instruction of hundreds of children in lock-step routines of drill and recitation. More commonly, graded schooling marked the distinction between country and town schools. It reflected not only the numbers of children to be schooled but also the possibility of employing more than one teacher and thus of the division of labor. In this respect, graded schooling was regarded as an instructional reform, allowing for more systematic and thorough teaching of material and assessment of student learning (Kaestle, 1973, 1983).

The significance of graded schooling for our purposes is that it created the problem of rational promotion or advancement. If schools were to be mass institutions organized hierarchically into classes or levels of instruction, what would be the grounds for determining when children were ready to move to the next class?

This brings us to a second aspect of "student accountability," academic standardization. Historically, systems of academic standardization developed largely in relation to the development of urban public high schools. Throughout the 19th century, public high schools were highly selective institutions. Even the largest cities supported only one or two such schools, which often enrolled fewer than a hundred students each. These students came from grade schools throughout a city or migrated to the city from town or country schools. This meant that students came from widely different school experiences. In order to determine the relative qualifications of such students, high schools administered admissions exams. From the perspective of high school principals and city superintendents, these examinations served not only to equalize the basis for admission to high school but also to establish a common standard of high achievement for lower schools. Schoolmasters throughout a city could assess the rigor of their instruction through the relative success or failure of their best students on high school admission exams (Labaree, 1988; Reese, 1995).

These points about the origins and perceived early significance of academic examinations are worth noting because they remind us that standardized examinations have always been more about schools than about students. Standardized examinations certainly mattered to individual students, as they determined their access to higher schooling. But the problem that conditioned the development of standardized exams was not differences among students but differences among schools. The problem of school differences is even more apparent in a third aspect of "student accountability" — the high school diploma.

The high school diploma originated in the 19th century not as a document with any legal standing but as a kind of marketing tool aimed at promoting school persistence. At a time when high school attendance was neither legally compulsory nor practically necessary, academies and high schools designed elaborate graduation certificates and exhibitions in an attempt to inspire students toward completing a full course of higher study. But what did such a certificate really mean? Again, the answer differed greatly from school to school. In particular, huge gulfs existed between the norms of operation in the large number of schools and academies in the countryside and the much smaller number of urban public high schools. Urban public high schools, with their much larger populations and funding bases, could afford to employ much larger, more specialized, and more qualified teaching staffs than could country schools. What's more, they could afford to be selective in the admission of students and strict in their assessment of performance. Not only the content and quality of instruction but the academic and social discipline enforced by urban public high schools far exceeded that contemplated by other schools (Reese, 1995).

Given this context, diplomas or graduation certificates from competitive urban public high schools clearly meant something different from those awarded by most academies and country schools. In the

1870s and 1880s, several states undertook efforts to standardize the meaning of the high school diploma. Together, groups of urban high school principals, university men, state legislators, and state education officials developed what could be called the first credentialing systems for high school education.

States took two main approaches to this task. Some states, such as Indiana and Michigan, focused on schools. They designated certain high schools as "commissioned" high schools. Diplomas granted by these schools guaranteed admission to state universities (Angus & Mirel, 1999; Stahly, 1998). Other states took a different approach to standardizing high school credentials. Instead of focusing on schools, they focused more directly on students. New York and Minnesota developed statewide achievement exams designed to assess individual student mastery of high school curricula. Students who met state standards of achievement across a full set of examinations received special diplomas issued directly by the state. These diplomas also gave students a certain standing within state universities (Beadie, 1999, 2000).

Now that we know something about the 19th-century origins of three elements of student accountability — graded schooling (and thus grade promotion), standardized examinations, and high school credentials — what can we learn from this history? Probably the most important thing we can learn is that the present is fundamentally different from the past. Although graded schooling endures, standardized academic examinations are enjoying a revival, and the meaning of the diploma is still in question, the conditions under which these systems operate have radically changed. These changes profoundly affect the moral significance and practical consequences of student accountability systems.

CHANGES IN THE HISTORY OF STUDENT ACCOUNTABILITY

To begin to appreciate what history can teach us about current accountability issues, we must first recognize fundamental differences between conditions of schooling in the late 19th century and conditions of schooling now. The most important and fundamental of these differences is that in the late 19th century only a small proportion of youth ever attended high school, let alone graduated. Calculating historical attendance rates is a complicated business that depends on how age cohorts are defined and whether the calculations include boys and girls, Blacks and Whites, North and South, public and private institutions. No matter how one defines the population base or the meaning of secondary school completion, however, high school students were a minority. For the United States as a whole, one set of estimates would put the high school enrollment rate between 8% and 10% in 1900 (Rury, 1991).

All this suggests the *voluntary* or *nonessential* nature of high school attendance in the late 19th and early 20th centuries. Although compulsory school laws were on the books in a few states as early as the 1870s, these laws were not enforced until after the turn of the century. More to the point, high school attendance was voluntary in *practical* terms. Apprenticeship and self-directed learning, bolstered by elementary common schooling and occasional periods of formal or semiformal instruction, were still legitimate and common paths of entry into all lines of work, including the professions. A year or two of high school study might commend a youth to some employers, especially in urban environments, but most youth and employers alike regarded work experience as a more valuable qualification than high school attendance or graduation (Kett, 1977; Rury, 1991). Not even colleges required that students attend high school. Despite some states' attempts to standardize the relationship between secondary and higher education through examinations or diplomas, admission to college in 1900 still occurred primarily by entrance examination (Beadie, 1999; Krug, 1969). The only thing for which high school attendance was a particular recommendation was school teaching—a fact that helps explain, in part, why most high school students in the late 19th century (55%–75%, depending on the setting) were women (Beadie, 2001).

Once we appreciate the small proportion of students who attended high school and the voluntary character of that attendance, we can begin to see how the academic standardization promoted by late-19th-century educators differed from similar efforts at standardization now. The standardized examinations and commissioned diplomas of the late 19th century belonged to a culture of aspiration rather than to one of minimum competency. Developed to address problems in the systematization of *higher* schooling, they provided incentives for individual students to achieve at levels above the norm for most children. They aimed, in other words, at *selectivity* rather than universality. The idea of late-19th century standardization was *not* to establish universal minimum standards whose achievement would be common to *all* children (*common* education, after all, was the business of *common* schools). Rather, the point was to confer honor and distinction on those *few* individuals who managed to persist through graded schooling and achieve at levels well beyond those expected or attained by the vast majority of the population.

This distinction between two kinds of standards—universal minimum competency and selective achievement incentives—is an important one often glossed over in current talk about performance-based standards. Caught up in the zeal of our conviction that *all* children can achieve high standards, we fail to recognize that, historically, these two kinds of standards have operated in different ways with different sets of consequences. Nowhere are these different sets of consequences more apparent and more significant than in the history of the high school diploma.

At the turn of the 20th century, the type of standard represented by a high school diploma was clearly that of an achievement incentive. If high school *attendance* was a minority experience, high school *graduation* was a rarity. For the United States as a whole, one set of estimates would put the proportion of youth who graduated from high school at 6.4% in 1900 (Green, 1980). If anything, these figures are high. No matter how the figures are calculated, however, the point is the same. To acquire a high school diploma at the turn of the 20th century was to achieve significant academic and social distinction. Moreover, the meaning and value of the diploma were directly related to the rarity with which it was achieved. The point of academic standardization in this context was to maintain the diploma's rigor and selectivity (Labaree, 1997).

Since the turn of the 20th century, the meaning and value of the high school credential have fundamentally changed. This transformation is the product of two trends that occurred at roughly the same time. Over the course of the century, high school education not only became more common; it also became more closely tied to the economy. Both these changes were actively promoted by reformers. In the 1910s, educators, business leaders, and politicians began deliberately pursuing higher rates of high school attendance and more direct ties between high schools and the economy. They did so through legislation such as the Smith-Hughes Act of 1917, which provided federal funding for secondary-level vocational education in commerce, industry, and home economics. They also did so through rhetoric such as the Cardinal Principles of Secondary Education of 1918, the National Education Association report that reframed the purposes of the high school in essentially nonacademic terms (Krug, 1969).

Many historians of education as well as current reformers are highly critical of the "watering down" of the academic content and purpose of high schools advocated by reformers in the 1910s (Angus & Mirel, 1999; Ravitch, 2000). They are also justifiably critical of the gender, race, and class bias that came to structure access both to the most rigorous academic content and to the most valuable vocational training offered by comprehensive high schools (Anderson, 1988; Tyack & Hansot, 1990). This line of criticism seems to suggest that we could and should turn back the clock to the model of the rigorously academic high school that existed in leading cities in 1900.

To consider the implications of this line of criticism, we must examine the long-term consequences of changes advocated by reformers in the 1910s. Initially, these effects were modest, but they cumulated over time. With regard to graduation, the proportion of the relevant age cohort receiving diplomas increased steadily from under 10% in 1910 to just under 30% in 1930 (Green, 1980). This trend accelerated in the following decades, particularly in the 1930s, when paid work became scarce (Angus and Mirel, 1999). By 1940, the proportion of youth receiving high school diplomas had risen to 50%, a tipping point that inaugurated a heyday of high school culture (Graebner, 1990; Green, 1980). The force of this change was apparent not only among youth but also among adults. Men and women who had not completed high school when they were youth enrolled in the huge adult education and training programs sponsored by schools in the 1940s and 1950s. By 1965, more than 75% of the population had a high school diploma, a ratio that has risen only moderately since (Green, 1980; U.S. Department of Education, 2002).[1]

One way of framing the significance of this dramatic change in rates of high school attainment is to say that the concept of "high school dropout" was invented in the 1950s. Educators had complained about the lack of persistence among high school students since the mid-19th century, but until the mid-20th century, this complaint only made sense in relation to the very small number of students who attended high school at all. Only in the 1950s did dropout begin to be seen as a "social problem" that policy makers ought to address (Dorn, 1993).

The "problem" arose not simply from changing social norms but from concurrent changes in the relationship between education and the economy. For a brief time in the 1940s and early 1950s, the idea of the comprehensive high school worked. During this heyday, the vocational education offered by machine shops and commercial departments in the best-equipped high schools proved to have real value on labor markets — at least for the White students that corporations, labor unions, and office staffs would admit on equal terms. This value is apparent in income data for high school graduates. As industry recovered from the Great Depression and expanded in the 1940s, a high school education began to produce economic returns in a way it had not before. Until 1940, high school attendance produced virtually no economic benefit to students as a group, at least in the short term, because most jobs were available to youth with or without high school educations. Male youth aged 18 to 24 who had attended high school earned roughly the same mean income as all youth in their cohort. Beginning in the 1940s, however, a significant income gap developed between those with and without high school educations. In 1949, youth with 1 to 3 years of high school earned 39% more than the mean for their age group. Those with a full 4 years of high school, meanwhile, earned 145% more than their peers. After 1949, the economic value of high school graduation continued to increase. More profound than the increased value of the high school diploma, however, were the increased costs of *failing* to graduate from high school. In 1974, the quarter of the population who did not graduate from high school earned incomes 700% below the mean for their age group, and the divergence between their incomes and those of graduates had increased to over 1000% (Green, 1980).

To summarize, the meaning of the high school diploma fundamentally changed between 1920 and 1970. This change had little to do with the academic content or rigor of high school curricula. It had everything to do with the extent of high school attendance and graduation in the population and the use of educational credentials to structure labor markets. In 1920, high school attendance and graduation belonged to the culture of aspiration. A diploma was an achievement attained by only a small minority of youth. In 1940, high school graduation became a norm rather than a rarity, and one that conferred considerable economic as well as academic and social benefits. By 1965, the high school diploma had become a necessity, with the liabilities of *not* acquiring a diploma becoming more important than the advantages conferred by having one. Since 1965, the financial benefits of graduating from high school have declined, but the consequences of *not* graduating from high school have become more and more profound.

It is worth taking a moment to appreciate more fully what these consequences are. The implications of earning an income several hundred percentage points below the mean may seem self-evident. We do not remind ourselves often enough, however, that in our society money is not just money but the means to acquiring virtually every other basic human good, including health and health care, food, clothing, and shelter. To fail to acquire a high school diploma in 1900 was no great matter—hardly anyone had one, and hardly any job or even any college admissions office required one. To fail to earn a high school diploma now, however, is to court human catastrophe. What was once an "achievement incentive" has become a "minimum standard," not simply for schooling but for survival in our society. This fundamental change in the economic and social significance of *not* acquiring a high school diploma is the reason we cannot simply turn back the clock to the academic high school of the past.

LESSONS FROM THE HISTORY OF STUDENT ACCOUNTABILITY

Now that we've recognized some fundamental differences between conditions of schooling in the late 19th century and conditions of schooling now, we can begin to use that knowledge to analyze current issues. From a historical perspective, the current push toward student accountability confounds distinctions between "achievement incentives" and "minimum standards." On the one hand, reformers have sought to *raise* academic standards and establish new "achievement incentives" in public education. They have done so by developing performance-based standards and statewide assessments that set the benchmarks of grade-level achievement at points well *above* those attained by many, or even most, students. At the same time, legislators and politicians have turned these new achievement incentives into "minimum standards" by making them a condition of high school graduation, a level of attainment currently expected of virtually all high school students. In the simultaneous use of the same benchmarks for two different kinds of standards lies a contradiction.

Education officials and legislators are not innocent of this contradiction. To a considerable extent they intend it. The prevailing wisdom is that by purposely raising standards above the norms that most students achieve and simultaneously saying that we expect all students to achieve them, we can effectively force both students and schools to do whatever it takes to make universal high achievement a reality.

If reformers and legislators are not entirely innocent of the tension they have created, however, they may be ignoring its likely consequences. History suggests at least two possible effects of current strategies. The first is that the pressure to achieve nearly universal graduation rates will lead to lowering standards to levels that the vast majority of students already achieve. The second is that the simultaneous pressures to raise standards and to achieve universal attainment will lead to multitiered systems of graduation, in which different levels of performance result in different kinds of diplomas.

Each of these scenarios has ample historical precedent. Consider the results of two attempts at standardization from early common school reform: efforts to standardize the length of the school year and efforts to standardize teacher qualifications. With respect to the length of the school year, the problem from the perspective of reformers was the small amount of schooling available to children in some districts. States thus focused on setting universal minimum standards. The difficulty with establishing a minimum standard, however, was the wide range of practices that existed across districts. At the same time that some schools operated just 3 months a year, most schools operated at least 6 months a year and many urban and town schools already operated for 11 months a year. To mediate this range of practices, many states set the standard at 5 months a year, a level somewhat below that already achieved by most schools (Swift, 1911). The goal, in effect, became one of bringing the poorest schools up to the standard that *decent* schools already achieved, thereby achieving a universal minimum standard. What resulted was a process of homogenization, but at a level lower than that which the most ambitious schools had once achieved. Over the course of the 19th century, the length of the school year in urban and town districts became shorter and the length of the school year in rural districts became longer, with schools eventually converging on a common standard somewhere in between (Gold, 1998).

This example reveals a fundamental dynamic of standardization. Historically, the viability of a minimum standard is directly dependent on the extent to which the standard has already been attained. The history of school reform is replete with cases that confirm this essential principle. With respect to school attendance, for example, it is clear that compulsory school laws were established and enforced only when and where universal attendance at the age and level they specified had already been nearly achieved (Tyack, James, & Benavot, 1987).

Recognizing this essential dynamic of standardization, states generally pursued a somewhat different strategy with respect to teacher certification. Again, the problem from the perspective of early common school reformers was the poor preparation of teachers in many schools. As early as the 1820s, most reformers advocated the equivalent of a normal school education for teachers. This amounted to a 3-year course that combined liberal arts instruction with special classes in pedagogy and experience assisting senior teachers. In setting standards, however, state officials could not simply legislate what they considered to be the best practice. Once again they had to consider the wide range of existing conditions. Whereas the most ambitious teachers already pursued advanced academic training, the vast majority of working teachers had little more than a common school education. To set the standard at the level of best practice would be to ignore the real dilemmas of existing schools. In reality, the demand for teachers was so great, and the supply of well-educated teachers was so low, that few districts, whatever their intentions, could hire teachers with advanced academic educations (Beadie, 2000).

In response to this dilemma, most states developed multitiered teacher certification systems. By this means, they effectively reconciled two competing goals. On the one hand, they sought to bring all teachers and schools up to a mandatory minimum standard. On the other hand, they encouraged schools and teachers to seek *higher* levels of education and preparation than those already commonly achieved. To address both these goals, states established certification systems that resulted in different kinds of certificates with different benefits and terms of renewal. Lower grade certificates had to be renewed more often, were good only for certain kinds of teaching, and were often not transferable from district to district. Higher grade certificates, by contrast, were good for life and throughout a state (Beadie, 2000).

Similar multitiered systems of certification also existed in some states with respect to high school graduation. When states first began regulating diplomas in the 1870s and 1880s, officials confronted a wide range of high school programs and standards of attendance, discipline, and achievement, with the most competitive high schools existing in cities. To address this range of conditions, states effectively developed multitiered systems of academic standardization. Some students received state-certified or "Regents" diplomas based on their attendance at "commissioned" high schools or their successful performance on state-standardized exams. Other students, meanwhile, continued to receive "local" diplomas based on whatever criteria their particular districts established for high school completion (Angus & Mirel, 1999; Beadie, 1999; Stahly, 1998).

These examples reveal a second dynamic of standardization. Historically, multitiered certification systems developed as a way of reconciling the goal of raising academic standards with the widely varying conditions under which schools actually operated. What is different so far in the current reform context is the refusal to acknowledge these variations. The assumption seems to be that differences in rates of academic achievement across schools are essentially a technical problem, and that the failure to resolve this problem is due primarily to a lack of will and expertise on the part of educators. From this perspective, the tension between raising standards and establishing minimum graduation requirements that is built into standards-based reform is its chief innovation. This tension will finally force educators and schools to confront their failures of expertise and commitment in a way that they have not done before.

This assumption is challenged by this book. Ken Sirotnik (2002) rightly points out that variations in rates of academic achievement across schools are deeply embedded in the inequalities and injustices of the larger society. He then asks whether it is ethically and educationally responsible for current accountability systems to place the entire burden for addressing those inequalities and injustices on educators:

> Just as educators need to be held accountable, so do policy makers and the public as a whole. A society that is still marked by substantial racism and classism cannot expect just and equitable public schools no matter how much rhetoric is heard about better leadership, better teaching, and "closing the achievement gap."(pp. 664-665)

A second assumption of current accountability systems is the efficacy of punitive measures for inducing positive change. The new accountability systems establish benchmarks not only for student improvement but for school improvement, and they threaten to exact consequences on schools that fail to achieve those benchmarks. The idea is that schools that consistently fail to produce academically successful students should ultimately lose their claim to public support, and that the threat of this loss of support will motivate schools to do more to help students succeed. In his critique of accountability systems, Sirotnik (2002) questions this proposition that "punishment and the threat of punishment" are "productive ways to change behavior either for individuals or for groups." Noting that research in behavioral psychology substantially refutes this notion, he wonders whether there is "something fundamental in the American psyche that gravitates toward punishment or the threat of punishment — a kind of 'spare the rod and spoil the child' ethic" (p. 667). (See also his discussion in the concluding chapter of this volume.)

As a historian I am reluctant to delve into such issues of social psychology. It is true, of course, that there is a history of discipline and punishment in American schools. It's also true that American public schooling has always been at least as much (or more) concerned with social order as with the mastery of academic content. Whether or not these practices have common psychic roots with current accountability reforms is beyond my capacity to assess. Without getting into psychic origins, however, history does provide evidence on the matter of the relative effectiveness of punishment as a means of promoting high school achievement.

It is hard to imagine any more punishing set of consequences for high school failure than those that exist today. And yet these consequences have not produced increased high school attainment. In fact, something closer to the opposite has occurred. Despite all the real and demonstrably negative consequences of failing or dropping out of high school, the proportion of the population that successfully completes a high school education has not increased appreciably since 1965. Before 1965, when high school attendance and graduation still belonged to the culture of aspiration, rates of attendance and graduation continued to rise. Once high school graduation became a necessity, however, and the consequences of dropout became catastrophic, the rate of attendance and graduation stabilized (U.S. Department of Education, 2002).[2] In other words, the greater the liabilities associated with not getting a diploma, the more stable the rate of graduation has proved. Judging from this evidence, the current policy of turning the new higher performance standards into minimum graduation requirements may prove to be not only a moral error but a strategic mistake. The history of student accountability suggests that if our goal is student improvement, we should be looking for ways to restore a culture of aspiration by *decreasing*, rather than increasing, the threat of punishment.

NOTES

1. Calculations of high school graduation rates vary according to how age cohorts are defined. Green (1980) defined cohorts narrowly as the ratio of high school graduates to 17-year-olds in the population and found the rate varied up and down between 74.6% and 77.8% between 1965 and 1975. For the last 3 years of this period he used data from the *Digest of Education Statistics,* yielding a figure of 76% for 1972. Currently, the U.S. Department of Education (2002) calculates "dropout" rates (rather than graduation rates) for youth aged 16 to 24. With this broader definition, they find dropout rates declined slightly from 15% in 1972 to 11% in 2000. Whether we calculate the rate at 76% or 85% in 1972, however, the rate has changed only slightly in the last 30 years, especially as compared with the previous four decades.

2. See note 1 above.

REFERENCES

Anderson, J. (1988). *The education of blacks in the south, 1860–1935.* Chapel Hill: University of North Carolina Press.

Angus, D. & Mirel, J. (1999). *The failed promise of the American high school, 1890-1995.* New York: Teachers College, Columbia University.

Beadie, N. (1999). From student markets to credential markets: The creation of the Regents Examination System in New York, 1864-1890. *History of Education Quarterly, 39* (1), 1-30.

Beadie, N. (2000). The limits of standardization and the importance of constituencies: Historical tensions in the relationship between state authority and local control. In N. Theobald & B. Malen (Eds.), *Balancing local control and state responsibility for K-12 education: 2000 yearbook of the American Education Finance Association* (pp. 47-91). Larchmont, NY: Eye on Education, for the American Education Finance Association.

Beadie, N. (2001, October). *Analyzing the impact of female student markets on the history of higher learning in the United States.* Paper presented at the annual meeting of the History of Education Society, New Haven, CT.

Dorn, S. (1993). Origins of the "dropout problem." *History of Education Quarterly, 33*(3), 353-374.

Gold, K. (1998, April). *Standardizing the summer school through state formation; school calendar reform in New York, 1840-1890.* Paper presented at the Annual Meeting of the American Educational Research Association, Chicago, IL.

Graebner, W. (1990). *Coming of age in Buffalo: Youth and authority in the postwar era.* Philadelphia: Temple University Press.

Green, T. F. (1980). *Predicting the behavior of the educational system.* Syracuse, NY: Syracuse University Press.

Kaestle, C. F. (1973). *The evolution of an urban school system: New York City, 1750-1850.* Cambridge, MA: Harvard University.

Kaestle, C. F. (1983). *Pillars of the republic: Common schools and American society, 1780-1860.* New York: Hill and Wang.

Kett, J. (1977). *Rights of passage: Adolescence in America, 1790 to the present.* New York: Basic Books.

Krug, E. A. (1969). *The shaping of the American high school, 1880-1920.* Madison: University of Wisconsin Press.

Labaree, D. F. (1988). *The making of an American high school: The credentials market and the central high school of Philadelphia, 1838-1939.* New Haven, CT: Yale University Press.

Labaree, D. F. (1997). *How to succeed in school without really learning.* New Haven, CT: Yale University Press.

Ravitch, D. (2000). *Left back: A century of failed school reforms.* New York: Simon and Schuster.

Reese, W. J. (1995). *The origins of the American high school.* New Haven, CT: Yale University Press.

Rury, J. L. (1991). *Education and women's work: Female schooling and the division of labor in urban America, 1870-1930.* Albany, NY: State University of New York.

Sirotnik, K. A. (2002). Promoting responsible accountability in schools and education. *Phi Delta Kappan, 83*(9), 662-673.

Stahly, T. (1998). Curricular reform in an industrial age. In W. B. Reese (Ed.), Hoosier schools: Past and present. Bloomington: Indiana University Press.

Swift, F. H. (1911). *A history of public permanent common school funds in the United States, 1795-1905*. New York: Henry Holt.

Tyack, D., & Hansot, E. (1990). *Learning together: A history of coeducation in public schools*. New Haven, CT: Yale University and Russell Sage Foundation.

Tyack, D., James, T., & Benavot, A. (1987). *Law and the shaping of public education, 1785-1954*. Madison: University of Wisconsin Press.

U.S. Department of Education, Office of Educational Research and Improvement, National Center for Education Statistics. (2002). *The condition of education*. Washington, DC: Government Printing Office.

CHAPTER 3

What Ought to Matter in Public Schooling: Judgment, Standards, and Responsible Accountability

Harvey Siegel

Public education in the United States is increasingly driven by a concern for *accountability*. We want to make sure that our teachers and schools are doing their jobs well and that our children are learning as they should, and to verify this, we hold them accountable. We do so largely by testing our students, and then making policy decisions concerning school funding, teacher pay, student promotion and graduation, and much else, on the basis of the test results. Testing, then, is part of a broad system of accountability, in which we establish policies concerning the consequences of our testing activities. Accountability concerns what we do with our various assessments and test results.

We often speak of "high-stakes" testing, in part because the use we make of test results has such a significant impact on the lives of students. Because that use is a function of our accountability policies, we can just as well speak of "high-stakes accountability" — our accountability policies and practices have enormous repercussions throughout the system, affecting students, teachers, administrators, basic funding decisions at the school, city, county, and state levels, and more. In what follows I will

Holding Accountability Accountable. ISBN 0-8077-4464-6 (paper), ISBN 0-8077-4465-4 (cloth). Prior to photocopying items for classroom use, please contact the Copyright Clearance Center, Customer Service, 222 Rosewood Drive, Danvers, MA, 01923, USA, telephone (978) 750-8400.

be concerned both with high-stakes testing itself and with the role it plays in broader systems of high-stakes accountability.

Why engage in high-stakes testing and accountability practices? There are many answers to this question: to monitor student perform-ance, to measure teacher and/or school effectiveness, to guide funding and other decisions, and so on. Some reasons for such testing are good; others are not. But a key question, not often asked, concerns the relation of testing and accountability to our considered educational ideals. In what follows I briefly discuss a relatively uncontroversial aim of educa-tion, namely, that of *fostering critical thinking,* after which I consider the degree to which current high-stakes testing and accountability practices and policies contribute to the achievement of that aim. I argue that although some current testing and accountability practices and policies are perfectly legitimate, many of them are largely inimical to the achievement of our most defensible educational ends.[1]

WHAT ARE OUR EDUCATIONAL AIMS AND IDEALS?

The history of educational thought is littered with suggested aims of education. The fostering of creativity, the production of docile workers or good citizens, the maximization of freedom or of individual happi-ness, the development of religious faith and commitment, and the fos-tering of ideological purity are just some of the many educational aims that have been proposed by serious educational thinkers.

This is not the place to offer a systematic analysis and evaluation of the multitude of proposed educational aims. Instead, I will briefly artic-ulate an aim that is widely accepted in our current educational *milieu*: that of *critical thinking*.

On the conception of critical thinking I have defended elsewhere,[2] the critical thinker is one who is *appropriately moved by reasons*. Critical thinking involves skills and abilities that facilitate or make possible the appropriate assessment of reasons; it involves dispositions, habits of mind, and character traits as well. Let us briefly consider these two dimensions of critical thinking in turn.

A critical thinker is one who has significant skill and ability with respect to the evaluation of reasons and arguments. For to say that one is *appropriately* moved by reasons is to say that one believes, judges, and acts in conformity with the probative or evidential force with which one's reasons support one's beliefs, judgments, and actions. A critical thinker must have, then, both a solid understanding of the principles of reason assessment, and significant ability to utilize that understanding in order to evaluate properly beliefs, actions, judgments, and the reasons that are thought to support them. This dimension of critical thinking may be called the *reason assessment* component of critical thinking.

There are at least two general sorts of principles of reason assessment: general, or subject-neutral principles, and subject-specific principles. General, subject-neutral principles are the sort that apply and are relevant to many different contexts and types of claim; their applicability is not restricted to some particular subject area. Principles of logic — both formal and informal — are subject-neutral principles, as are most of the principles typically taught in traditional critical thinking courses. Utilizing statistical evidence well, properly evaluating observational evidence and causal claims, recognizing instances of fallacious reasoning such as begging the question: All these involve subject-neutral skills and abilities of reason assessment. To the extent that a student/person is a critical thinker, she or he is the master of a wide variety of subject-neutral principles of reason assessment.

Unlike these subject-neutral principles, some principles apply only to rather restricted domains; in those domains, though, they are central to proper reason assessment. Such principles are *subject-specific:* They guide the assessment of reasons, but only in their local domain. The critical thinker must have some knowledge of the subject-specific principles operative in various domains in order properly to assess reasons in those domains; the grasp and utilization of subject-specific principles of reason assessment typically requires subject-specific knowledge as well. For example, in order to evaluate the claim that my symptoms provide evidence that I have malaria, I must know some medicine; in order to evaluate the claim that because the sun is in position *P*, I should use shutter speed *S*, I must know something about photography. The principle "Yellowish-tinged skin indicates liver malfunction" will properly guide judgments and decisions in the doctor's office but not in the banana section of the local produce market. In general, then, principles of reason assessment can be both subject-neutral and subject-specific, and the critical thinker manifests a mastery of both sorts of principle. This is because the ability to assess reasons and their warranting force is central to critical thinking.

In addition to skills, and grasp of principles, of reason assessment, the critical thinker must also have certain attitudes, dispositions, habits of mind, and character traits. This complex can be called the *critical spirit* component of critical thinking. It is not enough that a person be *able* to assess reasons properly; to be a critical thinker, she or he must *actually* engage in competent reason assessment and be generally disposed to do so. She or he must habitually seek reasons on which to base belief and action, and must genuinely base belief, judgment, and action on such reasons. She or he must, that is, be appropriately *moved* by reasons: Given that there are compelling reasons to believe, judge, or act in a certain way, the critical thinker must be moved by such reasons to so believe, judge, or act. She or he must have habits of mind that make routine the search for reasons; she or he must, moreover, be disposed to base belief, judgment, and action on reasons according to which they are sanctioned. The critical thinker must value reasons and the warrant they provide. She or he must, accordingly, be disposed to reject arbitrariness and partiality; she or he must care about reasons, reasoning, and the living of a life in which reasons play a central role.[3]

Thus far, I have tried to emphasize two points. First, reasons have *probative* or *evidential force* — that is, they support the beliefs or claims for which they are reasons to some degree or other — and the critical thinker must be proficient at evaluating the probative force of reasons (i.e., the degree to which they support the relevant beliefs or claims). This is required for the critical thinker to be *appropriately* moved by reasons. Second, reasons have what might be called *normative impact*: They guide rational belief, judgment, and action, and the critical thinker must be so guided if she or he is to be appropriately *moved* by reasons. Probative force and normative impact are both key features of reasons. They are each captured by this conception of critical thinking, according to which the critical thinker is appropriately moved by reasons. On this conception, both skills and abilities of reason assessment, and the attitudes, dispositions, habits of mind, and character traits constitutive of the critical spirit, are crucially important dimensions of critical thinking.

In *Educating Reason* (1988, chap. 3), I offered four reasons for believing that critical thinking, as just conceptualized, constitutes a fundamental educational ideal: respect for students as persons; self-sufficiency and preparation for adulthood; initiation into the rational traditions; and democratic living. I won't review the discussion of these four reasons here, except to say that in my view the fundamental justification for regarding critical thinking as an educational ideal is the first, moral one: Conceiving and conducting education in ways that do not take as central the fostering of students' abilities and dispositions to think critically fails to treat students with respect as persons, and so fails to treat them in a morally acceptable way.[4]

But it is worth pointing out, before leaving this section, that taking the aim of critical thinking seriously has important implications for citizenship and democratic society, because it suggests that matters of public concern be decided in free and open deliberation, on the basis of relevant reasons. In this respect taking critical thinking seriously as an educational aim is especially appropriate in democratic societies such as our own (Scheffler, 1989; Sirotnik, concluding chapter, this volume).

THE ALLEGED *ARBITRARINESS* OF JUDGMENT

What subjects or items of knowledge are worth studying and learning? What counts as acceptable, or unacceptable, pedagogy? How should we assess student learning? How should we assess our own educational practices? What should we do on the basis of those assessments?

Such questions as these, which are fundamental to the enterprise of schooling, are notoriously difficult to answer in a way that a clear and substantial majority of parents, teachers, and citizens find compelling. Part of the reason for the difficulty is that answering them requires appeal to *criteria*, which can themselves be controversial. For example, if a school board member argues that the high school science curriculum should include units on astronomy, but not astrology — or, more dramatically, evolution but not "creation science" — both fellow school board members and unconvinced parents might disagree that an appeal to the criterion of *contemporary scientific opinion* is legitimate, because that criterion will itself be challenged by those who think that it privileges the worldview of atheistic "secular humanism." Similar cases can readily be found of curricular controversy over literature/language arts curricula whose choice of texts (e.g., *Fahrenheit 451, The Adventures of Tom Sawyer*, or a book by Judy Blume) are made on the basis of criteria that are rejected by others. Different sorts of cases concern criteria involving student performance. For example, some hold, but others deny, that the ability to read at "grade level," or write "standard English," is an appropriate criterion for promotion or graduation.

Even if questions concerning criteria could be uncontroversially resolved, further difficult issues remain. Suppose, for example, that a community is agreed that one criterion for awarding a high school diploma is the ability to read. Once we agree that ability to read is a relevant criterion, we immediately face the question: *How well* must the student read in order to graduate? That is, what *standard* of reading competence must the student meet? What counts as "meeting" the relevant standard?

Questions concerning both criteria (i.e., the considerations deemed appropriate and relevant for educational decisions) and standards (the degree to which, or level at which, the criteria are deemed to have been satisfactorily met) are controversial. A key reason for this is that all such decisions seem to be a matter of *judgment*, and judgments such as these are often thought to be inherently and unavoidably *arbitrary*. As we have seen, at least two distinct sorts of arbitrariness threaten: arbitrariness concerning the determination of appropriate criteria, and arbitrariness concerning the determination of appropriate standards or levels at which the criteria must be met. All such determinations rely on judgment. Is such judgment inevitably *arbitrary?*

The short answer to this question is *no*: Both sorts of arbitrariness can be overcome. But they cannot be overcome in a way that will bring comfort to advocates of high-stakes testing and accountability. For judgments concerning both criteria and standards can be justified nonarbitrarily by relating them to appropriate educational aims and ideals. And judgments concerning those aims and ideals can themselves be justified nonarbitrarily, by appeal to relevant arguments concerning the nature and aims of education. But defenders of high-stakes testing and accountability practices defend those practices by appeal to educational aims and ideals that fail to be adequately supported by such arguments. The result is that such testing is defeated, not by arbitrariness, but by its resting on indefensible aims and ideals, and its concomitant failure to be informed by more worthy and fundamental ideals.

Let us consider this alleged arbitrariness of judgment concerning standards and criteria in the context of a particular test, the Florida Comprehensive Assessment Test (FCAT). Doing so will help us see that the real problem before us does not involve arbitrariness but rather the striking "disconnect" and incompatibility between our testing and accountability practices and our considered educational aims and ideals.

A BRIEF CASE STUDY: FLORIDA'S FCAT TEST

The FCAT[5] is a descendent of earlier *minimum competency tests*[6] (Florida Department of Education, 2001). It tests students in several areas and at several grade levels, and passing it is required for both promotion to the next grade (passing the reading portion of the test in grade 3 is required for promotion to grade 4) and receipt of a high school diploma. Its aim, as articulated by the Florida Commission on Educational Reform and Accountability and adopted by the State Board of Education, is to "assess ... student learning in Florida" in a way that will "raise educational expectations for students and help them compete for jobs in the global marketplace" (Florida Department of Education, 2001, p. 18).

Passing the FCAT requires meeting the standards articulated in the *Sunshine State Standards:*

> The FCAT content is derived from the Sunshine State Standards adopted by the State Board of Education. The Standards are broad statements of what students should know and be able to do, and they are subdivided into smaller units called "benchmarks." The FCAT measures certain of these benchmarks in reading, writing, and mathematics. (Florida Department of Education, 2001, p. 7)

The FCAT is now a central component of Florida's Student Assessment Program, the primary purposes of which "are to provide information needed to improve the public schools by enhancing the learning gains of all students and to inform parents of the educational progress of their public school children" (The 2002 Florida Statutes, p. 1). As the former Commissioner of Education of the State of Florida, Charlie Crist, put it, "It is important to remember that the FCAT is not an end in itself, but a means to an end. The result is an improved education for Florida's children and increased accountability for its schools" (Florida Department of Education, 2001, p. 2). Students are required to take the FCAT because

> Florida students are increasingly expected to display high-level learning and perform complex problem solving. Today, the job market requires people who are proficient in advanced mathematics and who can read and construct meaning from difficult and technical texts. The FCAT is given to measure achievement of the Sunshine State Standards that are being taught to and learned by Florida students. (Florida Department of Education, 2001, p. 5)

In the several passages just cited, a number of aims or purposes of the FCAT are mentioned. Its use is intended to

- Assess student learning.
- Raise the educational expectations of students.
- Enhance student job competitiveness.
- Ensure that successful students (i.e., those who pass the test) are minimally competent in reading, writing, and mathematics in virtue of their meeting the benchmarks set out in the Sunshine State Standards.

- Provide information needed to improve the public schools and the education students receive in them.
- Inform parents of the educational progress of their public school children.
- Increase accountability for Florida public schools.
- Ensure that successful students are proficient in advanced mathematics and can read and construct meaning from difficult and technical texts, because the "job market requires" such people.

There are well-known objections to high-stakes testing programs, most of which have been made regarding FCAT. One is that it is discriminatory, because members of certain groups fail the test at higher rates than others.[7] Another is that the FCAT has become so dominating a concern of school and district administrators, because student performance fundamentally effects school funding, that curricula are sacrificed and teachers required to "teach to the test."[8] A third is that such testing contributes to teacher demoralization and attrition, at a time when Florida is experiencing a severe teacher shortage. Although these objections are in my view extremely serious, I will not discuss them here. Instead, I want to focus on the just-cited explicit aims of the test.

These stated aims reveal a conception of the aims of education that is worth spelling out a bit. That conception is largely *economic:* The aim of public education in Florida is overwhelmingly to ensure that students are able to attain gainful employment and function adequately in the local, state, and global economies. The more specific content aims mentioned, such as meeting the benchmarks in reading, writing, and mathematics set out in the Sunshine State Standards, are justified in terms of the broader economic conception of the aim of education articulated: It is important for students to meet these standards, because if they don't, they won't be able to compete in the global economy in which they find themselves.

The rationale for the test is also importantly political: We require students to take the FCAT because we want to hold schools and teachers accountable, and we want to make sure that our tax dollars are well spent — that we taxpayers are getting our money's worth. But this political rationale is itself understood ultimately in economic terms. We hold schools accountable in accordance with our standards: Our schools are doing well enough when enough of our students pass the FCAT and other tests, because we think that passing the tests ensures that they have a reasonable chance of succeeding, or at least surviving, economically.

To be clear: I am not suggesting that the state of Florida explicitly or officially conceives of the aims of the FCAT, or of public education more generally, in wholly economic terms. As we have seen, several of the articulated aims of the FCAT involve noneconomic matters concerning levels of student mastery of specific subject matter, student expectations, and the like. But the offered rationale for such noneconomic aims is itself economic: It is important for students to achieve such mastery, because their successful functioning in the marketplace depends upon it.

This economic conception of the aim of education is *instrumental:* Do well in school so you can have a good job, and have a decent place in the state, national, and global economies when your school days are finished. Although there is perhaps nothing wrong with wanting students to have good jobs and the benefits that go with them, this is a remarkably narrow view of education. It is narrow in at least two ways.

First, it ignores the whole host of broad aims of education articulated in the history of educational thought. In doing so, it ignores widely acknowledged intrinsic (rather than the stated instrumental, economic) and more fundamental aims of education—for example, the enhancement of knowledge and understanding, the fostering of rationality and good judgment, the opening of minds and the overcoming of provincialism and close-mindedness, the enlargement of the imagination, the fostering of creativity, and so on.

I immediately concede that such aims as these are difficult to test for. But that they are is a weakness of our tests, not of the aims themselves. Israel Scheffler (1989) decries the too common practice of focusing on "externals," such as test results, "because they are easier to get hold of than the central phenomena of insight and the growth of understanding" (p. 90) that should be our primary educational concern; Scheffler urges us to keep our educational eye on those central phenomena, rather than casting our gaze on less important but more easily tested matters. And he cites a highly relevant passage from William James, to which defenders of high-stakes testing should pay particular heed:

> Be patient, then, and sympathetic with the type of mind that cuts a poor figure in examinations. It may, in the long examination which life sets us, come out in the end in better shape than the glib and ready reproducer, its passions being deeper, its purposes more worthy, its combining power less commonplace, and its total mental output consequently more important. (James, 1958, p. 101; cited in Scheffler, 1989, p. 91)

Richard Pring (1999) offers a more recent articulation of the point, with specific reference to the moral dimensions of education:

> The control of education by government of what children should know and how they should learn, sustained by an all-pervasive system of assessment, leaves little room within the schools for that deliberation of what is worthwhile and for that forming of a moral perspective which is essentially unpredictable, not to be captured in a detailed assessment profile....The grave danger is that, in making schools more "effective" in reaching the goals laid down by government and its agencies, this central moral goal of education finds no place. (p. 159)

And in words reminiscent of James and Scheffler, Pring tellingly suggests as well that tests and assessment and accountability regimes of the sort we have been considering "necessarily have to promote the trivial, for that alone is measurable, and to ignore that which is most important" (p. 165). Although the point may be somewhat overstated, because it has not been shown that only the trivial is measurable, Pring's insistence that a focus on testing tends to distract educational efforts from the most important educational matters is well worth our attention, for this does indeed appear to be a basic flaw of the FCAT and other current high-stakes testing and accountability efforts. The fundamental aims mentioned above are harder to test for and to measure than the knowledge and skills tested for by the FCAT, to be sure. But they are nevertheless our most fundamental aims. Losing sight of them and focusing our tests instead on more easily tested items is rather like looking for our lost keys under the streetlight even though we know we lost them in the poorly illuminated bushes.

Second, and perhaps more important, the instrumental, economic view of the aims of education underlying the FCAT conceives of students as little more than future "workers" or, more generously, future "economic agents" — as little more than cogs in an all-encompassing economic engine. In so doing, it manifests a wholly inadequate view of students, because it fails to recognize them as ends-in-themselves rather than as mere means, with interests other than the economic ones emphasized by their institutions of public education.

There is, of course, nothing wrong with a strong economy. But to see education in strictly instrumental, economic terms is to do a great disservice to students. It is to treat them immorally, because it fails to treat them with respect, as autonomous agents whose desires, needs, and interests ought not to be subordinated to economic or other imposed ends (Siegel, 1988, chap. 3).

It cannot and should not be denied that education is highly valuable instrumentally. It plays an important and productive role in securing a whole host of public goods, including its important contributions to fostering and maintaining community, civility, tolerance for alternative worldviews and ways of life, and, of course, a productive economy, among others. But education is not only instrumentally valuable. It is also *intrinsically* valuable, in virtue of its contributions to student knowledge, understanding, open-mindedness, independence of thought, and autonomy — goods that are good for their own sakes, independently of their acknowledged economic and social payoffs. It is this central dimension of education — and a corresponding view of students as persons rather than as merely economic agents — that a focus on high-stakes testing and accountability ignores.

The point is most easily seen by considering our earlier discussion of critical thinking. If our educational aim is to foster in students the skills, abilities, dispositions, habits of mind, and character traits of the critical thinker, an education focused on the aims articulated by the state of Florida, to which the FCAT is the means, would be at best an educational scheme sorely lacking in attention to those aspects of a student's education that are crucial to the achievement of critical thinking. There is a tremendous disparity between the conceptions of education offered by the state of Florida, in its articulated rationale for the FCAT, and those suggested by the ideal of critical thinking. For the former, education is essentially concerned with helping students to become competent masters of a range of linguistic and computational skills, able eventually to garner occupational skills sufficient for maintaining a place in the existing economic order. For the latter, education goes far beyond such considerations, by seeking to inculcate the skills, abilities, dispositions, habits of mind, and character traits constitutive of the critical thinker, and in so doing ensuring and honoring the student's autonomy. This is a far deeper, noninstrumental, conception of education and its aims.

That education should be concerned with fostering students' autonomy is a philosophically very important point, one that has enormous practical ramifications as well. In an education that takes autonomy seriously, we do not strive to determine students' future life trajectories, for we take that to be the prerogative of the student, and we recognize that the years of public education end far too quickly for such determination. Indeed, in so far as we embrace that aspect of the ideal of critical thinking that highlights student autonomy and self-sufficiency, we recognize that students' futures are essentially always open. We educate so as to enable the student to *create* her or his future, not to submit to it (Siegel, 1988). The aim of education is not to shape the mind of the student, or to prepare the student for predetermined roles in the social and economic orders. It is rather to *liberate* the mind, by enabling the student both to envision possibilities and to evaluate their desirability intelligently (Scheffler, 1989, pp. 143–144). It is far from clear that an education built upon the economic, instrumental conception of the aims of education will do much to further that liberatory end. And it is striking that such noninstrumental ends play no discernible role in the state of Florida's educational thinking.

I do not mean to argue that the FCAT, or high-stakes testing more generally, is inimical to critical thinking. I have no doubt that some of the knowledge and skills for which the FCAT tests are of positive value from the point of view of the development of critical thinking. But I do want to suggest that that ideal is given very short shrift in an education focused on high-stakes testing and driven by accountability concerns. In such an education, the autonomy of the student and the liberation of the student's mind are largely ignored. The degree to which a student emerges from such an education as a critical thinker is neither an aim of education to maximize nor of testing to reveal. The instrumental, economic aims of education that the FCAT strives to foster and to measure are exceedingly narrow, and shallow, as judged from the vantage point of philosophical reflection on education and its proper aims.

CONCLUSION:
RESPECTING JUDGMENT AND TAKING IDEALS SERIOUSLY IN THE PURSUIT OF RESPONSIBLE ACCOUNTABILITY

So, is the FCAT arbitrary? Perhaps, but not in a problematic way. Although the establishment of precise pass/fail levels is a matter of judgment, and in that unproblematic sense arbitrary, the knowledge and skills articulated by the Sunshine State Standards, taught in the classrooms of Florida public schools and tested for by the FCAT, are not arbitrary. The weakness of those standards, and their associated content and tests, is rather that they are informed by a very narrow and philosophically uninformed vision of the aims of education. A well-educated person is much more than a person who is able to function successfully in the marketplace. But the latter is, for all intents and purposes, the full substance of the well-educated person conceived by the state of Florida and its educational visionaries. It is the paucity of that vision that renders the FCAT problematic. The narrow conception of education and its aims presupposed by the FCAT, and by other similar high-stakes testing and accountability initiatives, is inadequate. So, therefore, is the education for which the FCAT and similar tests are the chief measures of minimal competence.

From the point of view of critical thinking, the problem with the FCAT is not arbitrariness. The problem, rather, is that the FCAT and the broader system of accountability in which it is embedded are inadequate and indefensible — both as educational practices and as embodiments of a serious conception of education. Responsible assessment and accountability must be informed and guided by our richest, deepest, and philosophically most defensible educational ideals. Its failure to be so informed and guided is the FCAT's most fundamental flaw.

I trust it is clear that I am not arguing against testing, or accountability, per se. Responsible assessment of student learning and understanding is educationally both legitimate and important. But *responsible* assessment and accountability must be conducted in a way that furthers, or at least does not frustrate, our considered educational aims and ideals (Sirotnik, 2002). High-stakes testing and accountability efforts, like Florida's FCAT, unfortunately do not further our efforts to graduate students who are good critical thinkers. Indeed, they are typically conducted without any attention either to that or to any other defensible and fundamental educational ideal. This is the basic flaw of much educational practice, including that involving high-stakes testing and accountability like the FCAT.[9]

NOTES

1. I do not in what follows address more general questions concerning the ethics of testing and grading. For an excellent discussion, see Curren, 1995.

2. See Siegel (1988; 1997; 2003) and Bailin and Siegel (2003). The following several paragraphs are taken, with some changes, from the introduction to Siegel (1997).

3. I offer an account of thinking dispositions in Siegel, 1999.

4. This alleged justification is obviously "Enlightenment" or "Modernist" in its individualistic orientation, just as the conception of critical thinking allegedly justified by it is equally modernist in its valorization of rationality. Criticisms of this dimension of my conception of critical thinking, and the case for regarding it as a fundamental educational ideal, are systematically addressed in Siegel (1997, Part 2), Siegel (2003), and Bailin and Siegel (2003).

5. In what follows, the information concerning the FCAT presented is taken from the state of Florida's, and especially the Florida Department of Education's, own publications and web resources. I am grateful to my student Ana Cristancho for help in finding, evaluating, and assembling these and other relevant resources.

6. It is consequently not surprising that the FCAT shares many of the prob-

lems that plagued the earlier minimum competency tests, including those involving alleged arbitrariness (see Siegel, 1988, chap. 7).

7. African American students do significantly less well on the FCAT exams than Hispanic American students, who in turn do significantly less well than White non-Hispanic students. For some relevant data, see Florida Department of Education (2002, pp. 10-13). At the time of writing (May 2003), the press reports that more than 12,500 Florida high school seniors — mainly African American and Hispanic American — are expected to leave high school without obtaining their diplomas because of their failure to pass the FCAT, despite their having met all other requirements for graduation. In addition, more than 40,000 third graders in Florida (approximately 23% of the total) will not be promoted to fourth grade because of their failing FCAT scores. Needless to say, the issue is politically extremely contentious.

8. The state of Florida vigorously denies that FCAT encourages teachers to "teach to the test"; anecdotal and other data (including, at the time of writing, the experience of my daughter about to complete eighth grade) suggest otherwise. For the state's defense, see Florida Department of Education (2001, p. 6) and other documents posted at the Florida Department of Education web site.

9. Thanks to Ana Christancho and Ken Sirotnik for helpful advice on earlier drafts. I dedicate this paper to Don and Barbara Arnstine and the late Jim McClellan, three friends who have taught me much about the deficiencies of high-stakes testing. I regret my failure to address important problems caused by the *standardization*, and neglect of *individualization*, imposed by such testing. For brief discussion, see Sirotnik (2002, pp. 666, 669-670). Sirotnik's call for systems of accountability to "honor the professional judgment of educators" (p. 669) and his project to develop a more effective approach to "responsible accountability" are, I think, extremely important. These matters are addressed again in the concluding chapter of this volume.

REFERENCES

Bailin, S., & Siegel, H. (2003). Critical thinking. In N. Blake, P. Smeyers, R. Smith, & P. Standish (Eds.), *The Blackwell Guide to the Philosophy of Education* (pp. 181–193). Oxford, UK: Blackwell.

Curren, R. (1995). Coercion and the ethics of grading and testing. *Educational Theory, 45*(4), 425–441.

Florida Department of Education. (2001). *FCAT briefing book.* Available from http://www.firn.edu/doe.

Florida Department of Education. (2002). Technical report for operational test administrations of the 2000 Florida Comprehensive Assessment Test. Available from http://www.fldoe.org.

James, W. (1958). *Talks to teachers on psychology; and to students on some of life's ideals.* New York: Norton.

Pring, R. (1999). Neglected educational aims: Moral seriousness and social commitment. In R. Marples (Ed.), *The aims of education* (pp. 157–172). London: Routledge.

Scheffler, I. (1989). *Reason and teaching.* Indianapolis, IN: Hackett.

Siegel, H. (1988). *Educating reason: Rationality, critical thinking, and education.* New York: Routledge.

Siegel, H. (1997). *Rationality redeemed?: Further dialogues on an educational ideal.* London: Routledge.

Siegel, H. (1999). What (good) are thinking dispositions? *Educational Theory, 49*(2), 207–221.

Siegel, H. (2003). Cultivating reason. In R. Curren (Ed.), *A companion to the philosophy of education* (pp. 305–319). Oxford, UK: Blackwell.

Sirotnik, K. A. (2002). Promoting responsible accountability in schools and education. *Phi Delta Kappan, 83*(9), 662–673.

Sunshine State Standards. Available from http://sunshinestatestandards.net/

The 2002 Florida Statutes. Title XLVIII, K–20 Education Code, Chapter 1008, Assessment and Accountability. [Law about the FCAT.] Available from http://www.flsenate.gov

Standards for What? Accountability for Whom? Rethinking Standards-Based Reform in Public Education

Pedro A. Noguera

With the passage of the No Child Left Behind (NCLB) Act, public schools across the United States are for the first time required to show evidence that all of the students they serve are learning. For those unfamiliar with the ways in which the educational system has operated and functioned prior to the enactment of the new law, this may come as a surprise. For many years, the great shame of public education in the United States was that large numbers of students graduated from school possessing limited skills and knowledge. The new law is intended to ensure that all students demonstrate measurable evidence of academic achievement, and the slogan — Leave No Child Behind — dramatically captures this intention.

NCLB AND THE PROMISE OF AMERICAN EDUCATION

As noble and important as such a goal might seem, accomplishing it will be far more difficult and complicated than President Bush and sup-

Holding Accountability Accountable. ISBN 0-8077-4464-6 (paper), ISBN 0-8077-4465-4 (cloth). Prior to photocopying items for classroom use, please contact the Copyright Clearance Center, Customer Service, 222 Rosewood Drive, Danvers, MA, 01923, USA, telephone (978) 750-8400.

porters of the law may have imagined. Across the country, there are thousands of schools that have never shown any evidence that they can educate the majority of children they serve (Maeroff, 1988). Under the new law, such schools will be labeled "failing," and if they are unable to improve within a fairly narrow time frame, they face the prospect of being shut down or being subjected to various negative sanctions (Schwartz & Robinson, 2000).

For the most part, the most troubled public schools have traditionally served the children of the poor. This is especially true in large cities such as New York, Chicago, and Los Angeles, but it is also true in small cities like Compton, Poughkeepsie, and East St. Louis. In fact, wherever poor children are concentrated, especially poor children of color, public schools are almost always very bad. Of course, part of the problem is that owing to local financing, considerably less money is spent on the education of poor children (Barton, Coley, & Goertz, 1991), but it is also true that poor children are more likely to attend schools with fewer qualified teachers and inferior facilities (Darling-Hammond, 1997).

Middle-class and affluent children have almost always received a better education, one designed to ensure that they would retain and perhaps even surpass the achievements of their parents. But for poor children, especially minority children in the inner city, public education like public housing and public hospitals has rarely been associated with exceptional service and excellence. Rather, public schools that serve the poor have been more often associated with a litany of problems—high dropout rates, low test scores, discipline problems, and the like—and rarely have they been a source of hope and genuine opportunity for the children served.

Given the dismal state of so many public schools, the President's call to "leave no child behind" would seem to be a bold and significant development in educational policy. How could any reasonable person oppose the idea that schools should be required to show some measure of success in carrying out the function for which they were created and produce evidence that children are learning? Such a goal is after all a central element of the "great promise" of American education, a promise that was first enunciated by Horace Mann, one of the early architects of public education from Massachusetts. Mann called for schools that would serve as the "great equalizer of opportunity" and "the balance wheel of the social machinery." He envisioned this great leveling process occurring in a "common school" where the children of farmers and bankers, commoners and aristocrats would be educated together (Cremin, 1988, pp. 8–10). His vision called for schools that would ensure that an individual's status at birth would not determine what he or she could accomplish or become later in life. It is a vision and promise that has been intimately connected to the American Dream, and it was so powerful a source of inspiration that over time it led this nation to be the first modern democracy to create a system of public schools (Katznelson & Weir, 1985).

TAKING THE EASY WAY OUT

Advocates of the new law argue that it aims to make this promise real (Schwartz & Gandal, 2000). In compliance with NCLB, states across the country have adopted new academic standards and assessments designed to hold schools and students accountable for academic achievement. To ensure that a high school diploma is regarded as a legitimate indicator of educational accomplishment to colleges and employers, students in several states are being required to pass "high-stakes" exit exams prior to graduation. In the lower grades, students will not be allowed to advance from one grade to the next unless they have demonstrated minimal competence on standardized tests. Additionally, schools with high rates of failure will be targeted for various forms of intervention, and face the prospect of being taken over by state governments if they fail to improve (Elmore, 2003).

In many states, the new standards constitute a significant increase in the academic expectations that students are required to meet. They are rigorous, demanding, and not surprisingly many schools and districts are struggling with the challenge to meet them. They are struggling in part because they have never been expected to use high academic standards as a basis for teaching all children before, and they are struggling because many schools lack the essential ingredients to meet the needs of the children they serve. For example, schools serving recent immigrants who speak little or no English are held accountable to the same standards as schools serving native-born English speakers. The same is true for schools serving poor children with significant social and psychological needs (e.g., housing, nutrition, health, learning disabilities, etc.), and schools that are faced with shortages in essential resources (e.g., certified teachers, capable administrators, adequate facilities and learning materials). In the name of equity and the goal of "ending the tyranny of low expectations," all schools are being held to the same standards.

For obvious reasons, schools that were struggling before the new law was enacted are under the greatest pressure. Such schools are now required to demonstrate steady improvements in tests scores on state exams, or they face the prospect of being subjected to various sanctions imposed by the state. Under the new law there is no provision to provide assistance to struggling schools or to ensure that they will receive help developing the capacity needed to meet the needs of their students. Instead, what they will receive is pressure, and lots of it. The operating assumption behind the new law is that pressure and in some cases public humiliation are effective ways of forcing schools to improve.

In contrast, most schools serving affluent student populations begin this process with designations as higher performing schools. They too must produce evidence of incremental improvements for all of their students, but they are less likely to be threatened with punitive sanctions. In several areas of the country, it is now customary for local newspapers to rank school districts by the test scores of students. In most cases, the districts serving the most privileged students are at the top, whereas those serving the poorest children are at the bottom of the test scores ladder. This is hardly surprising. In fact, school rankings often follow a form of race and class profiling—if you know the demographic composition of a school or district, it is easy to predict where that school or district will fall on the rankings. This was true before NCLB, so it is not surprising that it is true now. However, never before have policy makers construed labeling schools and districts as "failing" as a strategy for improvement and reform (Noguera & Brown, 2002).

The advent of standards-based reform has drawn greater attention to the so-called achievement gap: the gaping disparities in student performance that correspond closely with racial, linguistic, and socioeconomic differences among students. Such patterns have been evident in school districts throughout the country for many decades, but because NCLB requires that test scores be disaggregated by race and released to the public, the issue has garnered considerably more attention recently (Noguera & Akom, 2000). Gaps in achievement are particularly noticeable in affluent suburban districts. As their scores have been released to the public, it has become evident that many communities that have had a reputation for sending large numbers of students to elite colleges and universities have a far worse track record with their minority students, even when there are very few of them and most of them are middle class (Noguera, 2001a). The achievement gap is now widely regarded as one of the major challenges confronting public education today, but once again, relatively little is being done to provide concrete assistance to the schools that need the most help.

As a result of NCLB, we now have high standards imposed on students but no standards for schools. State governments have not set minimal standards that schools must meet with respect to the qualifications of teachers, the state of facilities, or access to learning materials. Moreover, there is no effort afoot to ensure that schools provide students with an education that meets the new high standards. Although students are required to pass rigorous exit exams, schools are not required to ensure that all students have been adequately prepared so that they have the opportunity to learn the relevant material.

The irony of this situation warrants close examination. It would be analogous to the Food and Drug Administration setting standards for product quality by punishing individuals who consume faulty products, or the Federal Transportation Commission setting new standards for air safety and enforcing them by punishing passengers for security violations at airports. The absurdity of such an approach is obvious when we apply the logic of standards and accountability to other areas of service. Yet there has been relatively little outcry over the fact that students — who have no control over the quality of education they receive — are the primary individuals held accountable under the new law. In Florida, where numerous reports have exposed severe overcrowding in schools serving the poorest children, the state has taken the bold step of placing letter grades on the front of school buildings so that all can know a failing school even before they enter. Of course, the state still allows failing schools to operate, but they pretend that by labeling such schools with a "D" or an "F" on the front door (I actually visited a school with a "FF" grade in Miami), they have taken tough action. In Florida and several other states, governors and state legislators have taken credit for raising standards without doing anything to improve the quality of education provided to students in schools where they know conditions are most severe.

Similar arguments can be made about the accountability strategy built into the new law. We now have tough systems of accountability for students, but none for adults — teachers, administrators, governors, and legislators. I recently asked the superintendent of a large urban school district who is a leading proponent of standards-based reform how many adults in his district would lose their jobs if hundreds of students did not receive a diploma in June 2003. With a puzzled look he responded, "Perhaps a principal or two from one of the failing schools." I posed the same question to members of the state legislature and to some of the individuals who have been the architects of these reforms, and on each occasion my question was met with the same puzzled look. How could it be that the only constituency that is being held accountable and that stands to lose something vital — namely, a high school diploma — is made up of students, whereas the only thing at stake for most adults is the possibility that they will be embarrassed by low test scores? At a time when teachers and qualified administrators are in short supply in many areas of the country, it is unlikely that mass firings could be used as a threat for pervasive failure. I would argue that given the difficulty involved in improving schools, such a strategy would not even be fair or productive. But how fair is it that students—the only constituency that lacks lobbyists and representation in the state legislature—are being held accountable by the new law? Perhaps it is because some students are actually regarded as expendable.

At the high schools I work with in Boston, where in some cases half to two thirds of the seniors will be denied a high school diploma, I hear anger and resignation among students and teachers. I speak with principals who readily admit that most of their students have not been adequately prepared to pass these exams. I also hear from anxious parents who hope desperately that at the last minute public officials will come to their senses and reverse the policy as they recognize the folly of their actions and the devastating consequences that will befall many students.

However, it now appears increasingly unlikely that there will be any reversal in policy. When the results of the last exam were released in March 2003, Massachusetts State Superintendent of Instruction David Driscoll announced triumphantly that 90% of high school seniors had passed the exam, and he boldly declared victory (Feddeman & Perlman, 2003). Boston College researchers, however, pointed out that the actual percentage is closer to 78% if one calculates the passing rate by measuring how many students entered the ninth grade in 1999, and how many will graduate with diplomas in 2003. Moreover, even if we accept the state's figures, the results mean that 1 out of every 4 Black students, 1 out of every 3 Latinos, and just over a third of all special education students will not receive high school diplomas this year (Haney, Madaus, & Wheelock, 2003).

Similar practices with similar results have been obtained in places like Texas and Chicago where high-stakes exams have been in existence longer (Hubert & Hauser, 1999). Mass failings in these places have not led to backpedaling or a change of course from policy makers. It is not a stretch to conclude that because the casualties of this policy are overwhelmingly poor children of color, politicians are generally not troubled by the outcomes. Even though large numbers of students will leave school lacking the skills and certification to obtain meaningful employment, there has not been much concern expressed. Certainly, some wring their hands and publicly lament the failure of so many students, but many others seem to find solace in their belief that only the undeserving—the lazy, the unmotivated, and the dumb—have been affected.

DOING THE RIGHT THING:
ADDRESSING THE NEEDS OF THE TOUGHEST SCHOOLS

Although politicians, corporate leaders, journalists, and others have generally hailed standards-based reform as the tough medicine needed to cure the ills of public education, those closer to the neediest schools and students have typically been less supportive about the effects of the new law. As thousands of students in states like California, Massachusetts, Texas, and Florida are faced with the prospect of being denied high school diplomas, a growing chorus of opposition is emerging to what some regard as a gross injustice against poor students. Will our society truly be better off if thousands of students are denied high school diplomas, unable to go to college and significantly less able to find decent jobs? This is one of many questions that the advocates of NCLB have not answered, except through their silence.

Opposition to standards-based reform should not be equated with a desire to return to the past, to the time when it was possible for students to graduate with meaningless diplomas, or to when too many schools showed little interest in promoting higher levels of learning and achievement. Rather, many of those who oppose the new law and the way it has been implemented want to see state governments do more to assist struggling schools and would like to see measures of achievement broadened beyond a narrow focus on test scores.

One frightening result of NCLB is that in pursuit of the goal of raising test scores, "failing" schools have been compelled to enact a number of measures that have actually undermined the education and social well-being of students. Faced with cutbacks caused by declining state revenues, many schools and districts have been forced to eliminate subjects such as art, music, and even science if they are not covered on standardized tests. Some have eliminated field trips, recess, and physical education to increase the amount of time available for test preparation (Kohn, 2000). In secondary schools, several students have been required to enroll in test preparation courses, some of which meet for nearly 2 hours per day, in the hope that such a strategy will make it possible for more students to pass the exams. Rather than taking steps to ensure that students in failing schools are taught in enriched learning environments and exposed to creative and effective teachers and stimulating curricula, the narrow pursuit of higher test scores has reduced the focus of education to test preparation in too many schools.

What many advocates of standards-based reform fail to see is that it is possible to raise academic achievement and improve public education without compromising the quality of education that children receive. For this to happen, the scope and purpose of NCLB would have to be broadened considerably so that a variety of approaches could be taken to address the needs of poor children and struggling schools. In the remaining pages, I outline what some of these approaches might include in the hope that the debate over standards-based reform can move beyond critique to consideration of measures that might genuinely make a difference.

1. Respond to the nonacademic needs of poor children.

There are a few things that we know from research about the achievement gap. For example, disparities in achievement correspond closely with other disparities that exist in our society (Miller, 1995; Noguera & Akom, 2000). The students who are least likely to achieve in school are the students from the poorest families — the kids who are least likely to have educated parents, stable housing, or adequate health care. Put more simply, the achievement gap is a reflection of the socioeconomic gap, the health gap, and the gap in opportunity.

If we want to ensure that all students have the opportunity to learn, we must ensure that their basic needs are met. This means that students who are hungry should be fed, that children who need coats in the winter should receive them, and that those who have been abused or neglected receive the counseling and care they deserve. If the commitment to raise achievement is genuine, there are a variety of measures that can be taken outside of school that will produce this result. For example, removing lead paint from old apartments and homes and providing students in need with eye exams and dental care are just some of the steps that could be taken. This may seem obvious, but although the new law is called No Child Left Behind, many of these needs have been ignored, and consequently many children are being left behind.

Even without a major change in social welfare policy, it should be possible to use several successful models of full-service schools to provide poor students with the services they need (Dryfoos, 2001). Such schools provide a variety of services to the children and families they serve, including preschool, after-school programs, health services, and job counseling for adults (Eccles & Gootman, 2002). Given that schools that serve the poorest children are most likely to need assistance in providing these kinds of services, policy makers will have to take the lead in forming partnerships with social service agencies. It is not fair or reasonable to expect schools to meet these needs or to do this work on their own. This is a wealthy nation, and as in other affluent societies, it should be possible to ensure that all children here have access to the services they need so that they can concentrate on learning in school.

2. Hold state governments accountable for maintaining high standards in schools.

Just as we do for the maintenance of highways and the public water supply, we should ensure that common standards of service are upheld at all public schools. Unlike the state of Florida's government that affixes letter grades on schools as a symbol of the quality of education provided there, state governments should be required to ensure that no students attend schools staffed by unqualified teachers or learn in buildings that are falling apart. State governments should be required to establish minimal operational standards for public schools, and they should be held accountable for the quality of education provided to all children.

Historically, there has been very little focus on quality control in public education. Students who are behind academically are typically placed in remedial programs, some of which are supported by Title I funds from the federal government, but it is rare for districts to ensure that the programs are effective and that there is evidence that students are actually being helped. These programs must be evaluated so that we can be sure that we have not relegated the neediest students to programs that cause them to be further behind and fail to address their academic needs.

3. Focus on the problems facing low-performance schools.

Low-performing schools tend to be racially segregated, and they generally serve the poorest children (Orfield & Eaton, 1996). Such schools also tend to have high turnover among staff, particularly among administrators. At many high-poverty schools in California, large numbers of teachers are uncredentialed and lack training in the subjects they teach (Darling-Hammond, 1997). Low-performing schools also tend to suffer from a dysfunctional culture where low expectations for students, lack of order and discipline, and poor professional norms are common.

These schools need help, not humiliation. They need policies that ensure they can attract and retain highly skilled professionals. State governments in partnership with colleges and universities should devise intervention strategies to assist struggling schools. There is much research available on high-performing, high-poverty schools (Jerald, 2001; Sizemore, 1988) and on programs that have proven successful for raising achievement (Traub, 2002). Drawing on this research, intervention teams should be deployed to work closely with teachers, administrators, and parents in failing schools to create conditions that lead to improvements in teaching and higher levels of achievement. Such an approach will not lead to immediate improvement in achievement measures but should begin the process of gradually turning low-performing schools around.

4. Make schools more responsive to the parents and families they serve through the enactment of systems of mutual accountability.

One of the reasons schools in middle-class communities tend to perform well is that the parents they serve are empowered to insist upon high-quality education. Middle-class parents tend to have a clear sense of what a good education is, and they generally have the wherewithal to make sure that their children get one, even if it means pulling their kids out of mediocre or failing schools as the last recourse (Nocera, 1991). NCLB contains provisions to allow parents to remove their children from failing schools but without funds for transportation or access to information on superior alternatives. Poor parents are much more likely to defer to the decisions made by the professional educators who serve them, and they are more likely to accept the schools they are assigned to even if they are not happy with the education their children receive (Noguera, 2001b).

Poor parents constitute a captured market in public education; they typically have no option or choice but to accept what they are provided. When educators know that a constituency has no ability to challenge how it is being served, where does the incentive come from to serve it well?

The only way to ensure that poor parents are treated as valued consumers is for districts to devise strategies to ensure that the concerns and satisfaction of parents are taken into account in operations. Ideally, this should take the form of systems of mutual accountability in which the responsibilities of schools, parents, and students are clearly spelled out so that all can be held accountable for their role in the educational process. Some schools have attempted to do this through the formation of site councils that involve parents in decision making (Noguera, 2001a), and through the formal contracts that establish norms and expectations for school officials, parents, and students and are signed by all parties.

5. Implement diagnostic assessment to strengthen the link between teaching and learning.

In most states, standardized tests are used for ranking purposes; test scores are used to make comparisons between students and schools, not to figure out how to help those in need. Typically, state exams are given in the spring and the results are not available until the fall. By this time, students have been assigned to new teachers, and in some cases, new schools. Such an approach limits the possibility that data generated from the tests could be used to provide teachers with an accurate sense of the academic needs of students. It also makes it difficult to use data from the tests to make modifications in instruction.

Diagnostic assessments administered at the beginning of the school year can provide schools with a clearer sense of the strengths and weaknesses of students. Such an approach would make it possible for schools to monitor student performance over time and to measure the performance of students in relation to established standards. Provided with a clearer and more accurate sense of the learning needs of students, schools would be in a better position to make informed decisions about curriculum and instruction, and how best to utilize supplemental resources (e.g., Title I funds, grants, etc.). Schools should strive to ascertain how much academic growth occurs over a course of a year so that they can determine whether the approaches they utilize to support teaching and learning are effective. This requires treating assessment as an ongoing process of evaluating student knowledge and ability, not through the administration of more standardized tests but through meaningful analysis of student work.

It is common for teachers to assert that it is not fair to expect them to produce dramatic gains in achievement in a single year. Even the most gifted teachers cannot take students who start the year reading at the third-grade level and bring them to the ninth-grade level in a year. However, all teachers should be able to demonstrate that they add value to the knowledge and skills possessed by students, and that during the course of a school year their students experienced some form of academic growth.

This kind of accountability requires not only a change in assessment but, even more important, a change in the way we typically think about teaching. Too often, teachers see teaching and learning as disconnected activities. This is especially true in high schools where teachers are regarded as subject-matter specialists and perceive themselves as hired to cover material within a set curriculum. They see their job as teaching the material and the students' job as learning it. Such an approach to teaching makes it unlikely that teachers will take responsibility for the learning that is supposed to take place in their classrooms. It also reduces the likelihood that significant gains in achievement will occur, because teachers see their work as only remotely related to student learning outcomes.

A substantial body of research shows that higher levels of learning and achievement are most likely to occur through improvements in the quality of teaching (Ferguson, 2000). When teachers are fully invested in learning and when they base their effectiveness on the academic growth of their students, they will routinely look for evidence that the instruction they provide is enabling their students to acquire the knowledge and skills deemed important. When teaching and learning are connected in these ways, the ultimate evidence of teacher effectiveness and student learning is the quality of work produced by students. Ideally, this should also be reflected in higher test scores and a variety of authentic indicators of learning and achievement.

6. Build partnerships between schools, parents, and the communities they serve.

There is a vast body of research that has established the importance of parental involvement in raising levels of academic achievement (Epstein, 1991). Yet, although the advantages of constructive partnerships between parents and schools are clear, it is often the case that such partnerships have been difficult to bring about in low-income areas. In poor communities, tensions and strains often characterize relations between parents and schools, and distrust and hostility tend to be more common than cooperation in pursuit of shared goals.

Given the importance of parental involvement, it is imperative that schools devise strategies to establish partnerships based upon respect and recognition of mutual need. Several programs, such as the Comer school reform model (Comer, 1987), the local site councils in Chicago (Wong, Anagnstopoulos, Rutledge, Lynn, & Dreeben, 1999), and the use of formal contracts between parents and schools, have proven effective as strategies for engaging parents in constructive partnerships with schools. Such approaches should be encouraged as a matter of policy, both to address the captured-market problem described previously and to develop the kinds of relationships between parents and schools that are essential for academic achievement and the welfare of students.

Beyond parents, schools serving poor children and communities will often need other sources of help in meeting their needs. In many communities, help could be provided by private businesses and corporations, community organizations and nonprofits, churches and local government — organizations that have a vested interest in the health and well-being of the communities in which they are located. Some of these organizations may have no prior experience working with schools, and they may need to be persuaded to play a role in supporting public education and to do more than simply make token donations. To address the lack of resources that is common to urban public schools, strategic partnerships with other organizations should be developed to provide schools with technical support, material resources, and personnel to assist schools in meeting student needs.

A partnership developed in Pomona, California, provides an excellent example of how this can be done. This district straddles two counties — Los Angeles and San Bernardino — and because of its shared jurisdiction, it had been neglected for years by both local governments. About 10 years ago, the district decided to purchase a large shopping mall that had been abandoned and had become an eyesore. Using school bond money, the district purchased the property to generate revenue and to enhance its ability to help the families it serves. Serving as the anchor tenant, the district then began to lease property at the mall to private businesses and nonprofit organizations that provide child services. It also decided to locate the district personnel office at the mall to recruit new teachers. Today the mall is a vibrant youth services center. It generates revenue for the district, and the service organizations housed there provide services to youth and families in the district.

This kind of strategic partnership requires vision and imagination. It also requires creative use of resources, and know-how to successfully manage relationships between public and private organizations. A recent publication of the National League of Cities (2002) encourages local governments, especially municipal leaders, to play a greater role in developing these kinds of partnerships. Similar calls have been made by researchers and policy makers who recognize that improving public schools will require a higher level of civic engagement than previously observed in most communities (McLaughlin, 2000; Stone, 2001).

CONCLUSION

The movement for standards-based reform has succeeded in getting educators and policy makers to focus their attention on the need for schools to find ways to raise student achievement. There is evidence that it is forcing schools that were previously complacent to become more serious and coherent in how they approach teaching and learning; for the first time, many school districts are being forced to prove that they can educate all of the children they serve. These are not insignificant accomplishments. However, pressure alone will not produce substantial improvements in public education, particularly in communities with the greatest concentration of poverty. Schools serving poor children need help, and thus far the advocates for standards-based reform have not displayed a willingness to provide the help that is needed.

The six recommendations that I have outlined represent my estimation of the type of policy initiatives and concrete assistance that is needed by schools in poor communities. In putting these recommendations forward, I have avoided the impulse to suggest changes that are necessary but politically unviable. For example, if we were serious about leaving no child behind, we would make sure that all children in the United States would be covered by health insurance. As basic and important as this need might be, I recognize that, at the moment at least, there is no political will to bring this needed reform about. Given this unfortunate political reality, I have tried to be pragmatic and I have limited my recommendations to initiatives that are politically feasible. That does not mean that making them happen will be easy, but I do believe that it is essential to bring these issues into policy debates about standards and accountability.

Historically, when politicians contemplate how to "fix" public schools, they seize upon a fad or gimmick—a quick-fix solution that they hope will miraculously change public education (Tyack & Cuban, 1995). Among policy makers, the most popular reforms of the day include charter schools, vouchers, and testing. Less well known but no less influential are more substantive reforms, such as small learning communities and phonics-based approaches to teaching reading, that schools have pursued to solve their problems. Although some of these strategies and others have merit and have shown promise in some schools, no reform measure is likely to produce the wholesale improvement that is desired. This is because the educational challenges faced by poor communities are not merely educational—these challenges cannot be addressed in a vacuum. What is needed is a more comprehensive and ambitious approach to address larger environmental and societal challenges related to inequality, poverty, and powerlessness.

It is not fair or reasonable for our society to expect schools to solve the problems facing young people, especially those from poor families, without help. Unfortunately, that is the situation at the moment. I believe we must respond to this challenge by calling attention to the great injustice of the situation while simultaneously doing all we can to improve our schools.

The future of our society will ultimately be determined by the quality of our public schools. This simple fact has been understood throughout our nation's history. Finding ways to fulfill the great promise and potential of American education is the task before us. For the sake of the country, the kids, and our future, I hope that we can rise to meet this challenge.

REFERENCES

Barton, P., Coley, R.J., & Goertz, M.E. (1991). *The state of inequality*. Princeton, NJ.: Educational Testing Service, Policy Information Center.

Comer, J. (1987). New Haven's school–community connection. *Educational Leadership, 44*(6), 13–16.

Cremin, L. (1961). *The transformation of the school*. New York: Vintage Books.

Cremin, L. (1988). *American education: The metropolitan experience 1876–1980*. New York: Harper & Row.

Darling-Hammond, L. (1997). *The right to learn: A blueprint for creating schools that work*. San Francisco: Jossey-Bass.

Dryfoos, J. (2001). *Evaluation of community schools: an early look*. Available from http://www.communityschools.org/evaluation/evalbrieffinal.html

Eccles, J., & Gootman, J.A. (Eds.). (2002). *Community programs to promote youth development*. Washington, DC: National Academy Press.

Elmore, R. (2003). *Doing the right thing, knowing the right thing to do: The problem of failing schools and performance-based accountability*. Unpublished manuscript, Harvard Graduate School of Education, Cambridge, MA.

Epstein, J. (1991). School and family connections: Theory, research, and implications for integrating societies of education and family. In D. G. Unger & M. B. Sussman (Eds.), *Families in community settings: Interdisciplinary perspectives* (pp. 289-305). New York: Hayworth Press.

Feddeman, S., & Perlman, H. (2003, March 3). Romney announces MCAS retest results: 90 percent of class of 2003 have now passed. *Boston Globe*, p. 13.

Ferguson, R. (2000). *A diagnostic analysis of Black–White GPA disparities in Shaker Heights, Ohio*. Washington, DC: Brookings Institution.

Haney, W., Madaus, G., & Wheelock, A. (2003, March). *DOE report inflates MCAS pass rates for the class of 2003*. Retrieved April 4, 2003, from http://www.massparents.org/news/2003/inflated_scores.htm

Hubert, J., & Hauser, R. (Eds). (1999). *High stakes: Testing for tracking, promotion and graduation.* Washington, DC: National Academy Press.

Jerald, C.D. (2001). *Dispelling the myth revisited.* Washington, DC: Education Trust.

Katznelson, I., & Weir, M. (1985). *Schooling for all.* Berkeley: University of California Press.

Kohn, A. (2000, September 27). Standardized testing and its victims. *Education Week,* pp. 60, 46–47.

Maeroff, G. (1988). Withered hopes and stillborn dreams: The dismal panorama of urban schools. *Phi Delta Kappan, 69*(9), 632–638.

McLaughlin, M. (2000). *Community counts: How youth organizations matter for youth development.* Washington, DC: Public Education Network.

Miller, L. S. (1995). *An American imperative.* New Haven, CT: Yale University Press.

National League of Cities. (2002). *Municipal leadership in education.* Washington, DC: Carnegie Corporation.

Nocera, J. (1991, September/October). How the middle class has helped ruin the public schools. *Utne Reader,* 66–72.

Noguera, P.A. (2001a). Racial politics and the elusive quest for equity and excellence. *Education and Urban Society, 34*(1), 18–41.

Noguera, P.A. (2001b). The role of social capital in the transformation of urban schools in social capital and low income communities. In S. Saegert, P. Thompson, & M. Warren (Eds.), *Social capital and poor communities* (pp. 189–212). New York: Sage.

Noguera, P.A., & Akom, A. (2000). Disparities demystified. *The Nation, 270*(22).

Noguera, P.A., & Brown, E. (2002, September 24). Educating the new majority. *Boston Globe,* p. 21.

Orfield, G., & Eaton, S. (1996). *Dismantling desegregation.* New York: New Press.

Schwartz, R., & Gandal, M. (2000, January 19). Higher standards, stronger tests: Don't shoot the messenger. *Education Week,* 40-41.

Schwartz, R., & Robinson, M. (2000). Goals 2000 and the standards movement. In D. Ravitch (Ed.), *Brookings paper on education policy* (pp. 3-24). Washington, DC: Brookings Institution Press.

Sizemore, B. (1988). The Madison Elementary School: A turnaround case. *Journal of Negro Education, 57*(3), 37–62.

Stone, C. (2001). *Building civic capacity.* Lawrence: University of Kansas Press.

Traub, J. (2002, November 10). Does it work? *The New York Times,* pp. 8–15.

Tyack, D., & Cuban, L. (1995). *Tinkering toward utopia.* Cambridge, MA: Harvard University Press.

Wong, K., Anagnstopoulos, D., Rutledge, S., Lynn, L., & Dreeben, R. (1999). *Implementation of an educational accountability agenda: Integrated governance in the Chicago Public Schools enters its fourth year.* Chicago: Department of Education.

CHAPTER 5

Accountability for Adequate and Equitable Opportunities to Learn

Jeannie Oakes
Gary Blasi
John Rogers

On May 17, 2000, the 46th anniversary of *Brown v. the Board of Education,* a group of civil rights and pro bono attorneys filed a complaint in the California Superior Court on behalf of Eliezer Williams —
a student at Luther Burbank Middle School in San Francisco — and his peers across the state who lack "the bare essentials required of a free and common school education" (*Williams v. State of California*, p. 6). The plaintiffs assert that because Williams and thousands of other students like him are forced to attend schools without sufficient numbers of "trained teachers, necessary educational supplies, classrooms, even seats in classrooms, and facilities that meet basic health and safety standards" they are "deprived of essential educational opportunities to learn" (p. 6).

The *Williams v. State of California* (2000) complaint also argues that "the Constitution and laws of California require the State to ensure the delivery of basic educational opportunities for every child in California . . ." (p. 6) and that

Holding Accountability Accountable. ISBN 0-8077-4464-6 (paper), ISBN 0-8077-4465-4 (cloth). Prior to photocopying items for classroom use, please contact the Copyright Clearance Center, Customer Service, 222 Rosewood Drive, Danvers, MA, 01923, USA, telephone (978) 750-8400.

the State therefore has a nondelegable duty to ensure that its statewide public education system is open on equal terms to all and that no student is
denied the bare essentials to obtain an opportunity to learn. The deplorable
conditions at the schools the student Plaintiffs must attend fall fundamentally below even baseline standards for education. (p. 7)

In short, the *Williams* plaintiffs seek to hold state officials accountable for
the conditions under which California students are expected to learn,
particularly for the often shocking conditions in schools most likely to be
attended by poor children and children of color.

In what follows, we use the facts and arguments in *Williams v. State
of California* as examples as we reassert a fundamental principle of educational accountability. That is, responsible accountability systems must
attend to whether students have adequate and equitable opportunities
for learning. Although monitoring *what* students learn is certainly
important, it cannot be the sole element of a *responsible* accountability
system. To be responsible, an accountability system must also attend to
whether students have adequate and equitable opportunities for learning.

We say "reassert" because the coupling of adequate and equitable
opportunities to learn with rigorous content standards was central to the
appeal of early formulations of systemic educational reform (Smith &
O'Day, 1990). Yet, over the past 15 years, the push for "results-based"
accountability systems has effectively decoupled what states put into
their education systems and what they expect to get out of them.

The decoupling of student achievement from the conditions in
which students are expected to learn has led to accountability systems
that represent failures of opportunities as failures of merit. The result
has been accountability systems that seek neither to uncover nor to correct inequities in resources and opportunities and that hide the fact that
students who have fewer resources at school nearly always learn less at
school. Instead, such systems emphasize alternate explanations for outcome differences, including students' background characteristics, local
administrative mismanagement, or teaching incompetence.

To unmask and remedy that distorted view of students, teachers,
and schools, accountability systems must place students' access to educational conditions and learning opportunities side by side with their
achievement outcomes. They must also hold accountable everyone with
a role in the system—from elementary school students to governors. The
California case provides dramatic evidence of the fundamental shortcomings in "results-based" accountability as well as the ideological
underpinnings of those shortcomings. The debate and scholarship

around *Williams* also have led to a set of principles upon which more responsible accountability systems should be built.

SHORTCOMINGS OF "RESULTS-BASED" ACCOUNTABILITY

The problems highlighted in *Williams v. State of California* — students forced to learn in schools with too few qualified teachers, insufficient textbooks and instructional materials, and overcrowded, unsafe buildings — are simply not addressed in today's "results-based" accountability systems. For example, the accountability regime adopted by California in 1999 makes teachers and principals accountable to state officials. Yet they are accountable for one thing: average school and subgroup performance on the state's STAR test (a norm-referenced basic-skills test supplemented by items aligned with the state's content standards). The conditions under which teachers produce changes in test scores — the resources and instructional material they have, the size of classes, and the condition of their classrooms — are irrelevant. All of the consequences — positive and negative — fall without regard to the conditions teacher and students face or the resources they are given.

Conditions, Resources, and Opportunities Matter

Absent the right resources, conditions, and opportunities, students cannot be expected to learn the knowledge and skills for which they, their teachers, and their schools are being held accountable. Qualified teachers, relevant instructional materials that students may use in school and at home, and clean, safe, and educationally appropriate facilities enable students to acquire the knowledge and skills that the state has specified as important. They promote students' chances to compete for good jobs and economic security. They provide students with the tools to engage in civic life as adults.

A growing body of research demonstrates teacher quality affects student achievement and is particularly powerful for low-income and language-minority students (August & Hakuta, 1997; Darling-Hammond, in press). The textbook is recognized worldwide as a central tool of schooling, and numerous studies have documented a strong relationship between instructional materials and achievement (see Oakes & Saunders, in press, for a review). The condition of school buildings, including temperature, acoustics, and overcrowding, also influences students' educational experiences and outcomes (Earthman, 2002; Mitchell, 2002).

The consequences of not having adequate teachers, materials, and facilities are particularly harsh in high-stakes, standards-based education systems, such as that in California. Trained teachers and high-quality materials are important because they provide students access to the knowledge and skills required by the state's content and performance standards. Without them, students are unlikely to pass California's high stakes tests that determine grade-to-grade promotion and high school graduation. In sum, California's current accountability practices pose a double threat: First, the assessments can neither detect nor report inadequate resources; and second, the assessments exacerbate existing harms and add new harm.

Adequate Conditions, Resources, and Opportunities Can't Be Assumed

Much of the public, including policy makers, concedes that basic resources are important for students to succeed. Yet this concession is mitigated by a widespread belief that basic resources are available in all U.S. students' schooling experiences. Even as Americans decry the overall quality of schooling, they tend to take for granted that students are taught by qualified teachers, have sufficient curriculum materials, and attend schools with adequate facilities. For many, these are not seen as resources whose availability varies significantly among schools, or whose centrality to students' schooling requires examination, documentation, and defense.

In contrast to this assumption, an analysis of the data in the course of *Williams* found that a staggering number of California students do not have the teachers, materials, and facilities that are fundamental to their learning and that are enjoyed by the majority of students (Darling-Hammond, 2003; Oakes & Saunders, in press; Ortiz, in press). For example, more than 42,000 teachers were working in California's schools without full preparation or credentialing (Shields et al., 2001), more than in 25 other states combined (Kentucky, e.g., has about 42,000 teachers— total).[1] In addition to at least 38,000 California teachers working as pre-interns or holding emergency permits because they had not met the state's standards for content knowledge and teaching skills, more than 2,700 were working on the basis of waivers without ever having passed a basic skills test (California Department of Education, 2002). In some schools, well over half the staff were teachers hired through emergency permits and waivers.[2]

California schools also suffered significant textbook shortages (Oakes, 2002). Twelve percent of teachers in a 2002 survey had too few copies of textbooks to supply every student in their classes (Harris, 2002). If those 12% are teaching 12% of California's students (a not unreasonable conjecture), approximately 720,000 of California's 6-plus million students are in classrooms where teachers do not have enough books for all of them. Nearly a third of teachers reported shortages that make it impossible for students to use textbooks at home. An even larger proportion who work with English learners said they lack books and materials that make content knowledge accessible to their students. Significant percentages said that the texts and materials they do have are in poor condition or provide inadequate coverage of the state's content standards and that they have too few auxiliary materials (e.g., measuring tools, science laboratory equipment and supplies, novels and supplementary materials, internet access) (Harris, 2002).

As yet another example, many California schools are so overcrowded or physically deteriorated that learning is disrupted (Ortiz, in press). Although the state lacks data that reveal the extent of these facilities problems, facilities expert Robert Corley (2002) cites a federal General Accounting Office (GAO) study in 1996 concluding that 42% of California's schools had at least one building in "inadequate" condition. He cites a 2001 finding by the *California State Legislative Analyst* that, "Despite significant sums raised for school construction in recent years, about one in three California students attends an overcrowded school, or one in need of significant modernization" (Corley, 2002, p. 6). Corley estimates, conservatively, that if only 10% of the state's schools are in unusually poor condition, this would affect at least 400,000 California students.

Inadequacies Affect Most Heavily Low-Income Students of Color

The distribution of problems such as those detailed above tells a disturbing story of different and unequal opportunities to learn related to students' race, social class, and community. Academic programs, teachers, resources, and instructional materials are allocated in ways that systematically disadvantage low-income students, African American and Hispanic students, and students in inner cities. The California data make clear that students in high-poverty schools — disproportionately children of color and those still learning English — are those most challenged by overcrowded, deteriorating facilities. Their schools more frequently lack critical instructional resources. Often these are also schools with the fewest qualified teachers and the schools in which student achievement rates and numbers of students going on to college remain very low.

The proportion of California schools staffed completely with fully qualified teachers has increased in response to recent policy initiatives (from 24% in 1997–98 to 28% in 2000–01). Nevertheless, the share of schools in which more than 20% of teachers are underqualified has also increased sharply, from 20% in 1997–98 to 24% in 2000–01 (Shields et al., 2001, p. 20). The schools with these large numbers of underprepared teachers — about 1,900 schools enrolling more than 1.7 million children — serve mostly children of color, who frequently experience a parade of short-term, underprepared instructors throughout their school careers (Darling-Hammond, in press).

California schools with inadequate textbooks, curriculum materials, equipment, and technology are also more likely to be schools serving less advantaged students. Both the Harris (2002) survey and data collected in conjunction with the RAND study (Stecher & Bohrnstedt, 2000) of class-size reduction reveal that schools with high populations of students of color or students who are eligible for free or reduced-price meals offer students significantly less access to textbooks and instructional materials than do schools with lower populations of these students. For example, the RAND data show that 83% of teachers working at schools serving small percentages of low-income students reported that they always had access to textbooks, whereas only 57% of teachers at schools serving a large population of low-income students indicated that they always had access to textbooks.

Additionally, the Harris survey found that 22% of teachers in schools with more than 25% English learners reported that textbooks and instructional materials at their schools were only fair or poor, whereas only 14% of teachers in schools with lower percentages of English learners reported these inadequacies (Harris, 2002). Moreover, teachers with high percentages of English learners (more than 30%) in their classrooms are less likely than teachers with low percentages (30% or less) of English learners to have access to textbooks and instructional materials, in general, and materials needed by English learners in particular. Sixty-eight percent reported not enough or no reading materials in the home language of their children, and 29% reported that they did not have any or enough reading materials at students' reading levels in English. Teachers with high percentages of English learners were also almost twice as likely as teachers with low percentages of English learners to report that the availability of computers and other technology was only fair or poor (Gándara & Rumberger, in press).

As with shortages of qualified teachers and adequate textbooks and materials, schools with unusually poor facilities are most often found in communities where students are less likely to be fluent in English, more likely to receive free or reduced-price lunches, and more likely to be socioeconomically disadvantaged.[3] Even within the same school districts, Corley (2002, p. 10) observes that campuses with facilities problems are more likely to serve minority students, students who are less affluent, or limited English speakers. He also notes that the data in the Harris poll to this effect are consistent with his personal assessment. Only 4% of teachers in schools Harris identified as "low risk" on socioeconomic and language factors rated their school facilities as poor, compared with 18% of the teachers in schools where the risk factors were high.[4]

The uneven distribution of basic educational tools places the burden of the system's deficiencies squarely on the backs of low-income students and students of color. Absent standards and a monitoring system for resources, conditions, and opportunities, the accountability system simply punishes the victims. It identifies teachers and students who have inadequate conditions in which to teach and learn what the state expects. This misplaced blame must negatively affect public perceptions of students who attend the schools and make it harder to recruit and retain teachers for these schools (often students' lack of success is transferred directly to their teachers' personal failings rather than to the structures that encourage underpreparedness).

Such findings raise complex educational and political problems. Schools serving large concentrations of children from poor families, from African American and Latino families, or that are located in inner cities often lack the political clout to command resources equal to those of other schools. As a result, their students face greater obstacles than do their more advantaged peers as they attempt to meet the content standards the state has set, pass state tests that are required for grade-to-grade promotion and high school graduation, and qualify for competitive opportunities in college and the workforce. These poor conditions also breed social alienation and pose real threats to students' whose health and well-being are already vulnerable to the poverty and racism that pervade their lives (Fine, Burns, Payne, & Torre, in press).

SHORTCOMINGS OF ACCOUNTABILITY SYSTEMS THAT HOLD ONLY STUDENTS, TEACHERS, AND SCHOOLS ACCOUNTABLE

Under California's Public School Accountability Act (PSAA), the consequences of success or failure, determined by students' achievement scores, fall entirely on teachers, principals, and students. When (or if) the state actually denies high school diplomas to students who fail its High School Exit Exam, the impact will hit students and families with brute force. However, the accountability regime is blind to the performance of other actors in the system—even when these other actors are crucially important in determining the conditions in local schools and the opportunity students have for learning. The governor, legislature, superintendent of public instruction, state board of education, or local district officials are not held to account for anything (Blasi, 2002).

The absence of accountability for anyone above the level of the school reflects a prevailing assumption that all that is necessary to motivate teachers and students to improve student learning are rewards or punishments based on test score outcomes. This fails any real-world test.

Good teaching requires more than motivation and effort. If the teacher lacks knowledge and skills, commitment alone will be a disservice to students. Moreover, the results of teachers' knowledge, skills, and efforts are shaped by conditions over which they have little control. A struggling novice working with a small number of well-prepared students in a clean, modern facility, and with more than enough textbooks, workbooks, and other learning materials, may have students who test well—especially if he or she focuses on increasing test-taking skills. A highly experienced and effective teacher working in an overcrowded, unbearably hot classroom with students with very poor preparation and no books to use for homework may not have students who test so well. Should we then reward the former teacher and punish the latter? Should we extend those consequences to the principals of their schools? More to the point, should we punish the students of the latter teacher? Most would think not, but that is precisely the consequence of California's PSAA—and most test-based accountability systems in the United States.

Focusing solely on outcomes not only ignores the powerful empirical effects of the circumstances within which teachers try to teach and students try to learn; it also ignores the fact that many of the most important conditions are beyond the control of the school.

An exclusive accountability focus on teachers and principals could be justified only if teachers and principals had both the personal and the resource capacity to perform to the highest levels. Yet it is clear that teachers (especially in low-income communities of color) frequently lack what they need to help their students reach high levels of achievement. Principals must compete with other principals, and districts with other districts, for the scarce resource of talented, trained teachers. This competition is made more arduous when all that some principals can offer are workplaces that would, if they were housing, be condemned as slums.

In fact, the state is responsible for ensuring that districts have the facilities, qualified teachers, and materials and resources to enable schools to meet the school standards. Districts must ensure that those resources actually reach schools and students.

Under the existing regime, it is clear who pays the price when student test scores fall below expectations. But who (other than teachers and students) pays the price (read, *is accountable*) when there are no books, when defective heating or air conditioning makes both teaching and learning nearly impossible, or when a school cannot attract or retain teachers with even a minimal amount of training?

The answer to this question in California is simple: no one. There is no reported instance in which a district or state bureaucrat was denied a promotion because he or she had not seen to it that books were moved from a warehouse to the classrooms that needed them. Despite widespread reports of threats to the health of children (and the public) because of conditions in many school bathrooms, there is no reported case in which any adult—from janitor to district superintendent—was disciplined as a result. In fact, Los Angeles Superintendent Roy Romer simply denied the results of a recent TV news investigation exposing deplorable conditions in the bathrooms of Los Angeles schools. Rather than reacting with concern or a commitment to fix anything, Romer responded, "That's not characteristic of this district, that's just not a fair characterization of this district" (Paige, 2003).

SHORTCOMINGS STEM FROM IDEOLOGICAL DECISIONS, NOT TECHNICAL CONSTRAINTS

In 1989 President Bush and the nation's governors convened an Education Summit to respond to an educational crisis—some say real, some say manufactured. Despite the myriad efforts following *A Nation at Risk*, U.S. students continued to lag behind those in other countries. The summit, led by then-Governor Bill Clinton, called for bold national goals and aggressive state efforts. It articulated a growing consensus that reform must be systemic rather than piecemeal. This reform would entail: (1) establishing standards for what all students should know; (2) providing schools with sufficient teachers, tools, skills, and resources aligned to the standards; and (3) holding schools accountable for their results. Central to this "systemic reform" was the coupling of standards for what students must learn with a guarantee to students of adequate and equitable opportunities to learn. This guarantee would be met by setting rigorous "delivery" standards and by holding the system accountable for providing the inputs and opportunities required to teach and learn the content standards (O'Day & Smith, 1993; Smith & O'Day, 1990). Without such "delivery" standards in place, it would be illegitimate to hold schools and students accountable for meeting content standards (O'Day & Smith, 1993).

By the early 1990s, the argument for systemic reform appeared in major documents of the National Governors' Association, the Business Roundtable, and the Council of Chief State School Officers. It became the basis of major initiatives sponsored by the National Science Foundation, and the focus of several major philanthropic foundations. The reforms that followed, however, fell short.

Despite bipartisan support for systemic state policies following the 1989 summit, significant political differences lay just below the surface. Specifically, conservatives who for most of the 1980s had advocated "market" reforms in public schools mounted a vigorous campaign to eliminate "delivery" standards from systemic reform. For example, Tennessee Governor Lamar Alexander elaborated this view in the mid-1980s:

> Governors are ready for some old-fashioned horse-trading. We'll regulate less, if schools and school districts will produce better results. The kind of horse-trading we're talking about will change dramatically the way most American schools work. First, the governors want to help establish clear goals and better report cards, ways to measure what students know and can do. Then, we're ready to give up a lot of state regulatory control—even to fight for changes in the law to make that happen—if schools and school districts will be accountable for the results. . . . These changes will require more rewards for success and consequences for failure for teachers, school leaders, schools, and school districts. (Alexander, 1986, p. 3)

> No amount of lecturing by governors or regulations from state legislatures can improve public education as well as allowing parents to make marketplace choices. It would straighten public education right up. If no one buys Fords one year, the guy building them is fired and someone else is brought in to do the job. (Alexander, 1984/1991)

Following the 1989 summit, Alexander—then secretary of Education in the Bush administration—led a campaign to eschew systemic reform in favor of a market-based approach. Market-based reforms and the educational "horse-trade" became increasingly popular with neoliberals (most notably Bill Clinton), as well as conservatives, in part because they allowed politicians to advocate for education reform without significant new investments. These politicians worried about the high costs of "delivery" standards in the worsening economy of the early 1990s. Thus first to go were standards that would hold the system accountable for equitable resources and school conditions for all students.

In March 1994, President Clinton signed education reform legislation making opportunity-to-learn (OTL) standards voluntary. Few states volunteered. Instead, most states have developed standards in the form of grade-level benchmarks in traditional academic content areas, measured by standardized tests. Accountability has been made concrete by attaching "high-stakes" rewards and sanctions for students and teachers to test scores. Equity has been defined as closing the test-score "gap" among racial groups on basic reading and arithmetic skills. Adopting a market-oriented approach, many policy makers sought to encourage quality with deregulation and/or choice and competition. Parents, as consumers, would choose, on the basis of publicized test scores, whether to "buy" the education provided at their local school.

In fall 1997, "Steering by Results" (California Department of Education, 1998) articulated Republican Governor Pete Wilson's interest in focusing California education policy on high-stakes, test-based accountability. *EdSource*, an organization that positions itself "as an independent, impartial, not-for-profit organization" whose mission is to "clarify complex education issues," explained,

> Attempts to improve schools with both incentives and sanctions are decades old. But past efforts tended to focus on compliance with laws and institutional policies: schools, for instance, have to offer certain programs and ensure that students receive a specified minimum number of instructional minutes. The current school accountability effort differs in that it is concerned not with inputs, but with outputs. (*EdSource OnLine*, 1998)

Notably, the reauthorization in 2002 of the federal Elementary and Secondary Education Act (President George W. Bush's No Child Left Behind initiative) enacted the market-based, horse-trade approach to standards, accountability, and school reform into federal law.

WHAT SHOULD RESPONSIBLE ACCOUNTABILITY SYSTEMS INCLUDE?

To be sure, students and parents should be accountable—for things within their control: doing homework, arriving at school reasonably rested, adhering to reasonable and fair discipline. Certainly, a focus on teachers is well placed, given the importance of teachers in the learning process. But, as noted above, there is something both undemocratic and inefficient about holding students, parents, teachers, and principals accountable for test performance without any knowledge or concern about the conditions under which that performance was accomplished — conditions that ultimately are determined by officials in the state capitol.

A better accountability regime would turn this system on its head and make state officials accountable to students and their parents. It would treat students and parents as agents as well as objects of accountability. It would encourage students and parents to make their views known and look to them as valuable sources of information about both positive and negative aspects of their educational experiences.

In sum, accountability must be systemic and shared, accounting for conditions as well as outcomes and distributing roles, responsibilities, and rights across all participants in the state. Systemic and shared accountability requires:

- Clear standards or benchmarks against which actors in the system can be measured. These must be sufficiently inclusive to specify both learning outcomes students are expected to achieve and the resources and conditions necessary to support teachers and students to as they produce those outcomes.
- Unambiguous lines of state, regional, and district responsibility for ensuring that all students have the learning conditions and opportunities required by state standards. That is, the "buck" for providing decent conditions and opportunities must stop somewhere, preferably with the officials who have the control of essential resources.
- Valid, fair, and useful measures of student learning that sit side by side with accurate and trustworthy information — from inspectors (state or local, public or private) or from students, teachers, parents, and so on — about the conditions and learning opportunities at the classroom level. This information must allow policy makers and the public to assess whether inputs (as well as outcomes) are meeting expectations.
- Accurate information about the performance of the officials above the level of the school in providing the resources, conditions, and opportunities that learning requires, and the distribution of that information to those with the power and resources to act on it, including policy makers, the public, parents, and students.
- Mechanisms for holding schools, teachers, and students account-

able for outcomes, augmented with mechanisms that hold the appropriate officials at state, regional, and district levels accountable for learning resources and conditions. These should include procedures for responding to failures at the point at which the failure is caused, and incentives that will induce better performance by these actors in the future.

- Legitimate roles for local communities, parents, and students in holding the system accountable. They can share their own knowledge, in light of existing standards for resources and conditions, with school, district, and state officials. Nonprofit, community-based organizations, supported by the state, can help develop informed, engaged, and critical publics in all communities (Rogers, in press).

To be sure, developing such accountability systems poses considerable political and technical challenges. On the political side, defining standards and developing indicators of adequate and equitable opportunities to learn require a careful balancing of centralized responsibility for providing resources and capacity against local flexibility over the processes of teaching and learning. It also requires clarity about which actors (offices, departments, etc.) in the system are responsible for providing teachers and students with what they need—a clarity that many state educational systems now lack.

On the technical side, choices must be made about what state standards and accountability for opportunities to learn should include—for example, whether they should focus only on inputs or also on school and classroom processes. Moreover, new measures will be needed. It may be straightforward to count the number of teachers without certification or those who are teaching out of their content area. However, it is far more complex to measure whether the schools' facilities and materials are sufficient to provide students with access to the rigorous curriculum that meeting content standards requires. (See Elmore & Fuhrman, 1995; Guiton & Oakes, 1995; Herman & Klein, 1997; McDonnell, 1995; Oakes, 1989; Porter, 1995; Traiman, 1993.)

Questions of feasibility must also be addressed. For example, will the state need a massive school inspectorate, prowling the halls of 8,000 public schools to see that children have the basic tools they need for learning? The fact is that we know how to create and operate efficient systems of accountability when we really care about the consequences. Some involve centralized bureaucracies, but many rely on empowered customers, partnerships between government and private enterprises, and other approaches. For example, the state sets minimal public health standards for restaurants. However, there is no army of state inspectors visiting cafes and hot dog stands. That task is delegated to county (and sometimes city) health departments. Those that fail inspections are given time to improve or, in some cases, they are closed down. Some of those health departments issue public "grades" to restaurants, which empowers customers to add the power of their purchasing decisions to government incentives.

Or, to cite another example, California has a highly effective, decentralized system of regulating tailpipe emissions from automobiles. All inspections, however, are performed by private businesses, which are in turn licensed by the state. This model is in fact used in ensuring that new schools comply with earthquake safety and other building codes: The state architect sets standards and licenses private inspectors to ensure that new schools comply. Others have suggested doing away with the entire superstructure of public education above the level of the individual school, converting every school to a "charter school," and allowing the decisions of parents to drive the accountability of school-level personnel. There is no single necessary organizational structure or approach to a workable accountability system.

SYSTEMIC AND SHARED ACCOUNTABILITY RESTS ON LEGAL, POLITICAL, AND MORAL IMPERATIVES

Most state constitutions, including California's, place the obligation to provide a basic education to all students with the governor and other state officials who take an oath to uphold the state's constitution and faithfully execute its laws. State officials cannot escape their legal responsibility to the children of the state by blaming anyone else — including individual schools, teachers, and students. Even so, there is little likelihood that those at the top will hold themselves accountable for ensuring that all students have the resources, conditions, and opportunities they need.

In California, *Williams v. State of California* seeks a court order that will impose systemic and shared accountability. Importantly, the trial court has already agreed with plaintiffs that the state is obliged to set in place a system that will either "prevent, or detect and correct," significant educational deficiencies and inequalities. Thus there is a substantial likelihood that the courts will order the state to devise new systems of ensuring adequate and equal opportunities for learning. Such an order will be a significant political shock to California's educational and political system.

However, a victory in the courts will not be enough to transform the educational opportunities provided to poor children and children of color, although it might offer a good start. Fundamental change will require widespread political pressure that reaches the state's highest levels. Policy makers must recognize that it is morally indefensible and politically untenable to stand by while significant numbers of children (usually poor and of color) are disenfranchised from a quality of education being received by other (usually White and wealthier) students. Such recognition may require a pointed, loud, and perhaps even risky discussion about how accountability can and should provide the public with the tools and power to monitor the state's obligations. That discussion, like the accountability system that results, must engage grassroots organizations, advocacy groups, and ordinary citizens, as well as educators and policy elites.

CONCLUSION

In many ways, this chapter goes to great lengths to argue what is patently obvious to great numbers of school children and their parents as well as uncontested by nearly all observers of the education system. For children to be educated, they require basic educational tools—teachers, books, and safe, healthy, uncrowded schools. Teachers, books, and adequate school buildings are the staples of American teaching and learning. They are not usually thought of as educational resources or conditions whose availability varies significantly among schools, or whose centrality to education requires examination, documentation, or defense.

California has failed to provide basic educational tools to many, many school children. Most often these are children who are poor, non-English-speaking, African American, and Latino. It is unacceptable that the educational system would deprive any California child of these basics. It is reprehensible that those children most deprived educationally are also those whom society neglects most in other ways. It is unspeakable that no one is held accountable.

Accountability systems are instruments for improving educational practice, and, as such, they should influence policy-malleable conditions that contribute substantially to educational quality. Because basic educational resources such as quality teachers and instructional materials represent the building blocks for quality schooling, accountability systems must be able to ensure their provision.

Moreover, accountability systems are the state's primary instruments for communicating to the public what it can expect from schools. Parents and community members need to know what resources and conditions matter and whether students have access to them. By choosing to count certain conditions or outcomes, accountability systems communicate important ideas to the public about what the state values and what conditions state policies can affect.

Finally, accountability systems are instruments for distributing roles, responsibilities, and rights across participants in the state's education system. The democratic and moral imperative demands that this distribution be fair and inclusive. Including opportunity-to-learn in its standards and accountability system communicates a state's commitments to equality of opportunity, fairness, and due process. These commitments lie at the core of democratic education and democratic governance of public schools.

NOTES

1. http://www.teachingquality.org/resources/pdfs/NBCTtoSCHOOLS.pdf

2. Clearly, there is a multiplicity of attributes we look for in competent or "highly qualified" teachers. Coursework and supervised training leading to a "full" credential, although an imperfect proxy for all these attributes, is nevertheless a practical and policy-relevant means to guarantee at least a threshold of competence among the system's teachers. And, although simply holding a full credential does not guarantee high competence, when large numbers of teachers lack such credentials, serious alarm must be raised. That is why teacher credentialing must remain the standard—a stance not so different from licensing and credentialing in professions such as law, medicine, or cosmetology. For example, holding a license does not guarantee a physician's competence, but not holding one would be a significant disincentive for prospective patients.

3. Earthman, 2002, p. 5, citing U.S. Department of Education, NCES, June 2000.

4. Harris created what he called a "risk index," which was based on an evaluation of the percentage of students whose families were on CalWorks, the percentage who received free or reduced-price school lunches, and the percentage of English Language Learners (ELL). He broke down the data so that one could compare the results for schools in the higher-risk groups (those schools with the higher concentration of low socioeconomic status and ELL students) with those in the lowest risk group (schools with the lowest concentration of low socioeconomic and ELL students).

REFERENCES

Alexander, L. (1984). As quoted in "Excerpts From Alexander's Writings on Issues in Education," *Education Week,* January 9, 1991. Available at http://www.edweek.org/ew/ewstory.cfm?slug=10090059.h10&keywords=Alexander

Alexander, L. (1986). *Time for results.* Washington, DC: National Governors' Association.

August, D., & Hakuta, K. (1997). *Improving schooling for language-minority children: A research agenda.* Washington, DC: National Research Council and Institute of Medicine, Committee on Developing a Research Agenda on the Education of Limited English Proficient and Bilingual Students.

Blasi, G. (2002). Reforming educational accountability. In D. J.B. Mitchell (Ed.), California policy options 2002 (pp. 53–78). Los Angeles: UCLA School of Public Policy and Social Research.

California Department of Education. (1998). *Steering by results: A high-stakes rewards and interventions program for California schools and students.* Sacramento, CA: California Department of Education.

California Department of Education. (2002). California Basic Education Data System, Educational Demographics Office. Available from http://www.cde.ca.gov/demographics

Corley, R. (2002). Expert declaration of Robert Corley, *Williams v. State of California.* Available from http://www.mofo.com/decentschools/expert_reports/corley_report.pdf

Darling-Hammond, L. (in press). Access to quality teaching: An analysis of inequality in California's public schools. *Teachers College Record.*

Earthman, G. (2002). Expert report of Glen I. Earthman, Williams v. State of California. Available from http://www.mofo.com/decentschools/expert_reports?earthman_report.pdf

EdSource OnLine. (1998) Shifting the focus to learning: California's accountability debates. Retrieved February 25, 2003, http://www.edsource.org/pdf/FinalAccntbilityRpt.pdf

Elmore, R. F., & Fuhrman, S. H. (1995). Opportunity-to-learn standards and the state role in education. *Teachers College Record, 96*(3), 433–458.

Fine, M., Burns, A., Payne, Y. A., & Torre, M. E. (in press). Civics lessons: The color and class of betrayal. *Teachers College Record.*

Gándara, P., & Rumberger, R. (in press). The inequitable treatment of English learners in California's public schools. *Teachers College Record.*

Guiton, G., & Oakes, J. (1995). Opportunity to learn and conceptions of educational equality. *Educational Evaluation and Policy Analysis, 17*(3), 323–336.

Harris, L. (2002). *A survey of the status of equality in public education in California: A survey of a cross-section of public school teachers.* Washington, DC: Louis Harris and Associates.

Herman, J.L., & Klein, D.C.C. (1997). *Assessing opportunity to learn: A California example.* Los Angeles: National Center for Research on Evaluation,

Standards, and Student Testing (CRESST) CSE Technical Report 453.

McDonnell, L. M. (1995). Opportunity to learn as a research concept and a policy instrument. *Educational Evaluation and Policy Analysis, 17*(3), 305–322.

Mitchell, R. (2002). Expert declaration of Ross Mitchell, *Williams v. State of California.* Available from http://www.mofo.com/decentschools/expert_reports/mitchell_report.pdf.

Oakes, J. (1989). What education indicators? The case for assessing school context. *Educational Evaluation and Policy Analysis, 11*(2), 181–199.

Oakes, J. (2002). *Education inadequacy, inequality, and failed state policy: A synthesis of expert reports prepared for* Williams v. State of California. Los Angeles, CA: Institute for Democracy, Education, and Access.

Oakes, J., & Saunders, M. (in press). Access to textbooks, instructional materials, equipment, and technology: Inadequacy and Inequality in California's public schools. *Teachers College Record.*

O'Day, J. A., & Smith, M. S. (1993). Systemic reform and educational opportunity. In S. H. Fuhrman (Ed.), *Designing coherent education policy: Improving the system* (pp. 250–312). San Francisco: Jossey-Bass.

Ortiz, F. I. (in press). Essential learning conditions for California youth: Educational facilities. *Teachers College Record.*

Paige, R. (2003, January 30, 11:16 pm). *Dirty lessons.* Los Angeles: KCBS News.

Porter, A. C. (1995). The uses and misuses of opportunity-to-learn standards. *Educational Researcher, 24*(1), 21–27.

Rogers, J. R. (in press). The role of California's parents in insuring quality schooling for all. *Teachers College Record.*

Shields, P.M., et al. (2001). *The status of the teaching profession 2001.* Santa Cruz, CA: The Center for the Future of Teaching and Learning.

Smith, M.S., & O'Day, J. A. (1990). Systemic school reform. In S.H. Fuhrman & B. Malen (Eds.), *The politics of curriculum and testing, Politics of Education Association yearbook* (pp. 233–267). London: Taylor & Francis.

Stecher, B., & Bohrnstedt, G. (2000). *Class-size reduction in California: The 1998–99 evaluation findings.* Sacramento, CA: California Department of Education.

Traiman, S. (1993). *The debate on opportunity-to-learn standards.* Washington, DC: National Governors' Association.

Williams v. State of California. (2000, May 17). Superior Court of the state of California, County of San Francisco, No. 312236.

CHAPTER 6

The Double Bind of Civic Education Assessment and Accountability

Roger Soder

Montesquieu pays brief but careful attention to the relationship between schools and the political regime in Book 4 of the first part of *The Spirit of the Laws*. Monarchies demanded honor, and that is what schools should teach. Despotic governments necessarily demand servility, and that is what schools should teach. But it is in republican governments, Montesquieu tells us, that "the full power of education is needed" (1750/1969) to teach the virtues of responsible citizenship. The founders of the American republic and other concerned citizens took with great seriousness Montesquieu's assessment. They went to great lengths in exploring and advocating the connection between the preparation of a free people to maintain their freedom in a democratic society and the institutions that would be directed toward that preparation (Pangle & Pangle, 1993).

The demand for civic education has not abated over the last two centuries. The role of schools in preparing students for a democracy was a staple of political rhetoric. The demand continues in our time, as indicated by responses to the annual Phi Delta Kappa/Gallup Poll. For example, of seven specified school purposes in the 2000 poll, "to prepare people to become responsible citizens" was given top priority, ahead of other purposes such as "to help people become economically self-sufficient" or "to improve social conditions" (Rose & Gallup, 2000, p. 47).

Civic education—teaching students their moral and intellectual responsibilities as critical and informed citizens in a democracy—arguably is the central function of American schooling. Because of its centrality, civic education must be given extensive and sustained attention in any responsible system of assessment and accountability.

In what follows, I examine the rhetoric of civic education to determine the extent to which the centrality of civic education is matched by such extensive and sustained attention. I consider how past and present advocates of civic education programs have included in their advocacy either explicit or implicit approaches to assessment of those programs. I do not claim total inclusiveness; rather, I have included illustrative examples across the spectrum of ideology and approach, while expecting the reader to go elsewhere for a comprehensive presentation.[1] The question of interest here is how educators in a given classroom or school get some sense of whether students are indeed learning the lessons of civic education and are becoming prepared to be active and good citizens in a democracy.

I use "civic education" as a placeholder for the vast array of programs and curricula passing under the names of "citizenship education" and "education for democracy," as well as "civic education" itself. No specific definition for this placeholder is provided here: Defining "civic education" is in itself what constitutes so much of the arguments and claims and counterclaims.

CIVIC EDUCATION ASSESSMENT APPROACHES

Our examination might reasonably begin with a consideration of talk during the second decade of the 20th century. By this time, American public schools, particularly high schools, are beginning to enroll larger numbers of students and educators are beginning to talk of civic education in terms that might leave the founders a bit bemused.

A 1913 report prepared under the auspices of the Commission on the Reorganization of Secondary Education sounds the themes of civic education for the new century: "It is not so important that the pupil know how the President is elected as that he shall understand the duties of the health officer in his community" (Jones, 1913, p. 17). It was about this time that sociologist Franklin H. Giddings proclaimed that "high school education should make citizens not learners" (Kliebard, 1994, p. 15).

In 1926, the American Historical Association's Commission on the

Social Studies began an extensive examination of social studies, involving a series of reports and publications. The commission's final report, *Conclusions and Recommendations* (1934), took broad swings at prevailing assessment practices:

> In their efforts to measure environment, conduct, honesty, good citizenship, service, knowledge of right and wrong, self-control, will, temperament, and judgment, the testers are dealing with matters that are not susceptible of mathematical description. (p. 94)

Moreover, available tests "have provided no adequate substitute for the older forms of examination or for the living, informed, and thoughtful judgment of the competent and thoroughly trained teacher" (pp. 100–101).

A prescient observation on the implications of assessment and evaluation is provided by the Educational Policies Commission (1940) in *Learning the Ways of Democracy:*

> The importance of evaluation to education is fundamental and its influence is pervasive, for evaluation is more than a technique subordinate to the purposes of education. To an extent not often realized, evaluation influences the purposes, contents, and methods of education, and sets the goals for which students strive. The teaching practices in a school almost invariably tend to follow the lead of those evaluation methods which have the greatest prestige in that school . . . the use of inappropriate methods of evaluation may seriously limit or cripple the best of citizenship programs. (pp. 379–380)

In a 1945–1950 study of citizenship education in the Detroit public schools, Stanley Diamond and colleagues used a variety of tests in trying to determine the impact of participating in the district's civic education program, including the California Test of Personality, the Mooney Problem Check List, Iowa Tests of Educational Development, and the Cooperative Test of Social Studies Abilities. He concluded that there were no measurable improvements in the quality of citizenship but stressed that the reader should use "unusual wariness in the interpretation of these test results" (Diamond, 1953, pp. 182–183).

The report of the 1977 National Task Force on Citizenship Education includes but modest references to assessment. "The superintendent is charged with maintaining the quality of the civic education program of the schools. He must regularly evaluate progress in this area and remain alert to opportunities for expanding and improving the program" (Brown, 1997, p. 11).

The notion of civic education assessment moving beyond subject-matter knowledge acquisition is also suggested by Newmann (1975; 1977a; 1977b), Mehlinger (1977), and Conrad and Hedin (1977a; 1977b). Participation is seen as a key factor in being a good citizen, with assessment focusing on volunteer service, internships, social and political action, community studies, and student projects to improve the school or community.

Participation as a factor in civic education assessment and evaluation is argued as critical in a larger sense by Wehlage, Popkewitz, and Hartoonian (1973) with assessment thus "concerned with measuring the ability of schools to engage students in the testing of the knowledge they learn and in the developing of an awareness of the tentative nature of these ideas" (p. 768).

Remy (1980) provides some indicators for assessing student involvement in terms of the capacity to "identify a wide range of implications for an event or condition, identify ways in which individual actions and beliefs can produce consequences," and "identify one's rights and obligations in a given situation" (p. 24). Remy notes that states are developing programs to test for citizenship competencies:

> It may be very difficult to meaningfully test large numbers of students for important citizenship competencies and to interpret test results, once obtained . . . . Some of the most important citizenship competencies involve human relations and social skills which are difficult to measure using paper-and-pencil tests. Yet, at present, practical considerations all but require the use of paper-and-pencil tests in minimum-competency-testing programs. As a result, some of the most important citizenship competencies — making decisions, making judgments, working with others — are difficult to reliably and validly measure. When such testing is attempted, important competencies or objectives are often reduced to trivial aspects of the citizen role. The result is that schools, teachers, and programs are assessed in terms of those aspects of citizenship competence which can be easily be measured, even though the importance of what is being measured is inversely related to its measurability. (p. 48)

Others focusing on process and participation in civic education include Morrissett (1981), Ehman and Hahn (1981), Cornbleth, Gay, and Dueck (1981), Battistoni (1985), Longstreet (1989), and Mosher, Kenny, and Garrod (1994). Little specific attention is paid to matters of assessment, although Battistoni (1985) does argue that participation aside,

> public high schools must show a commitment to providing each student with the basic foundations of a liberal education, and must back that commitment up with competency testing to make sure that students can master basic educational problems. (p. 193)

Going counter to what I suggest is a general unwillingness to address specifics of assessment, Engle and Ochoa (1988) devote an entire chapter of their volume to "assessing learning for democratic citizenship." The curriculum advocated calls for teacher–student negotiations of content and learning experiences; as such, "it would be a contradiction to impose assessment techniques that are externally determined without also permitting students to participate as fully as possible in the determination of those assessment strategies" (p. 179). That is to say,

> if teachers impose assessment strategies unilaterally, they deny the opportunity for shared responsibility and foster an authoritarian rather than a democratic relationship with students. Such procedures make it clear to students that compliance with authority is still the order of the day. Further, such practices create a climate in which democratic problem-solving becomes as arbitrary and authoritarian as practices that might be found in dictatorial political systems. (pp. 179–180)

Accordingly, Engle and Ochoa advocate teacher–student "negotiated" assessment in four areas: knowledge and intellectual skills; commitment to democracy; political and group skills; and student attitudes toward public issues and citizen participation.

Knowledge and intellectual skills are to be assessed through student projects such as essays, debates, photographic essays, or dramatizations. Appraisal of classroom dialogue, "by the teacher, by a selected student acting as observer, by a teacher colleague, or by any combination of students and teachers" (Engle & Ochoa, 1988, p. 183), is another part of knowledge/intellectual skills assessment. Questions to ask center on who participates, listening skills, use of evidence and reason, lack of teacher domination, and focus on major issues. It is suggested that this assessment be conducted once a month or every 6 weeks; videotaping is proposed as a useful option. Finally, the teacher can use open-ended essay test questions, working with students to determine the pool of questions and the criteria for appraisal.

Some researchers and advocates focus on making civic education broader than the school (Boyte, 1994; Dynneson & Gross, 1991; Wexler, Grosshans, Zhang, & Kim, 1991). Boyte (1994) argues that what is needed is civic education for public agency, in which people "learn politics, understood as the give-and-take messy, everyday public work through which citizens deal with the general issues of our common existence" (p. 417).

Houser and Kuzmic (2001) present a critical political perspective and argue for rejection of a worldview that is "directly or indirectly responsible for the privileging within our society of individualism over community, of mind over body, of man over woman, and of humankind over other living and non-living organisms" (pp. 456–457). Similarly, Gonzales, Riedel, Avery, and Sullivan (2001) argue that the national standards used for the NAEP civics assessment focus on the "dominant liberal perspective" with little attention to obligations to community and group, while neglecting the "expanding role of women and minorities in civic and political life in the late 20th century" (p. 123). Neither Houser and Kuzmic nor Gonzales and coauthors discuss specifics of assessment and evaluation matters.

Tolo (1999) examined statewide civics assessments in seven states and concluded that if the state tests include assessment of some subject areas but not civic education, the focus goes to what is tested and civic education is overlooked or given a low priority. On the other hand, if the state includes specific assessment of civic education in its testing, then there is the usual double-edged sword of focus. As Tolo argues:

> Perhaps the most salient issue regarding civics assessment is how one assesses civic participation and civic dispositions. Testing civic knowledge, at least at a basic level, can be accomplished through a written test. How, though, does one assess the other components of civic education? Furthermore, if one cannot effectively assess civic skills and dispositions, is it worth testing civic knowledge by itself? (p. 147)

Tolo (1999) concludes that

> a test of civic topics that does not cover all the components of civic education, including the higher-order intellectual and participatory skills so vital to effective citizenship, leads school districts to give inadequate attention to these critical components. (p. 149)

He welcomes "accountability systems and measures that ensure a curricular emphasis on civic education that addresses civic knowledge as well as civic intellectual skills, civic participation, and civic dispositions." He sees such systems and measures as "the best way for civic education to gain greater support and prominence" (p. 150).

On the basis of observations of 135 social studies classrooms in Chicago, Kahne, Rodriguez, Smith, and Thiede (2000) found that when teachers were preparing students for the Illinois State Constitution Test, preparation that "comprises a substantial portion of the eighth grade curriculum," students were less likely to engage in "higher order thinking," or in "deep and disciplined inquiry," and "had fewer opportunities to experience democracy as a way of life." When teachers respond to the state-mandated testing policy, "they provide fewer rather than more opportunities to develop as citizens" (pp. 330–331).

Conover and Searing (2001) assessed the extent to which students are "developing the skills and motivation necessary to sustain regular political discussion" (p. 105). They asked about kinds of issues talked about, and how often; they also asked about extent of tolerance of groups students identified as one they disapproved of most. One part of the assessment focused on the role of the high school in contributing to students' sense of citizenship and nurturing their practice of it, as well as the extent that role can be changed, with attention to four elements of the school experience: "The sense of school community, the students' level of civic engagement in school and extracurricular activities, the level of political discussion at school, and the curriculum" (p. 108). *Community* was measured by assessing extent of identification with school community and sense of shared interests. Following notions of social networks creating social capital, *civic engagement* was measured by the number of groups students belong to. *Discussion* was measured by asking students how often they had discussions or serious conversations about political issues in school, classes, and after school, and with teachers. *Curriculum* was measured by asking students where they talked about civic education. Not surprisingly, students indicated most discussions were in classes in civics or government.

In recent years, the National Council for the Social Studies (NCSS) has adopted various position statements centering on aspects of civic education. In its 1997 statement, "Fostering Civic Virtue: Character Education in the Social Studies," the NCSS claimed that "students should both understand the nature of democratic principles and values and demonstrate a commitment to those values and principles in the daily routines of their private and public lives" (p. 225). Thus "a focus on knowledge and skills alone is insufficient for the task of civic education. Civic education must also foster civic character in citizens" (p. 226). The position statement argues for going beyond the formal curriculum. It is necessary to have a

> school environment consistent with the principles and core values of the ideal of civic virtue. . . . The hidden curriculum of the school has the potential to teach important lessons about authority, responsibility, caring, and respect. The principles and values underlying the day-to-day operations of the school should be consistent with the values taught to young people. [Moreover,] a school curriculum that attempts to teach values such as responsibility and respect is unlikely to be effective in the hands of teachers

who are irresponsible in the performance of their professional duties and disrespectful in their dealings with students. (p. 226)

Finally, in this consideration of assessment practices related to civic education, we examined five well-known supplemental civic education curriculum programs available to the schools.

We, the People . . . Project Citizen is an issues-based civic education program from the Center for Civic Education designed for middle school students. The class works together to identify and analyze a public policy issue and then collectively presents a portfolio on findings and an action plan. The supplemental program does not deal directly with individual student assessment but rather with the entire class process. The teacher's guide "does equip teachers with evaluation rubrics for both the students' written and oral performance" (Patrick, Vontz, & Nixon, 2002, p. 103), but the major focus is on "the entire process, from identifying community problems/issues through to the reflection component," which "is in and of itself an evaluation instrument" (M. Fischer, personal communication, September 13, 2002).

Close-Up (www.closeup.org) is a 30-year-old effort to involve students in various programs ranging from a one-day individual school program to learn about local, city, and county governments to weeklong programs involving students from across the state learning about state issues. Materials for *Close-Up* suggest little in the way of assessment and evaluation at the classroom or school level. Rather, student feedback provides indicators of how well participants thought the program met their needs.

Street Law (www.streetlaw.org) focuses on participatory education about law, democracy, and human rights. Begun more than 20 years ago, the program provides textbooks (e.g., *Street Law*) for high school programs as well as other guides for teachers and students. At the state level, *Street Law* has developed course outlines and curriculum materials with specific competencies; for example, the learner will "assess working relationships among law-enforcement agencies at various levels" (www.streetlaw.org/ncstate.htm). From the long lists of competencies, teachers are left to develop assessment and evaluation tools.

The *Constitutional Rights Foundation* (www.crf-usa.org) provides on-line lessons on selected topics, including the Bill of Rights, election-year issues, sports and the law, school violence, impeachment, and the like. Each on-line lesson provides outlines of issues and resources. There are many suggestions for class, small group, and individual activities. There is no explicit attention to assessment and evaluation. Each teacher will develop assessment and evaluation tools as deemed appropriate.

Kidsvoting (http://kidsvotingusa.org) focuses on encouraging students to become active and informed participants in the American democracy. Combining suggested classroom activities and community engagement, each of the several curricula available is designed to foster information-seeking skills, higher order thinking skills, empathy toward other people, and participation. Materials delineate learning objectives, preactivity preparation, details of activities, and questions. Assessment and evaluation tools are not provided but will be developed by individual teachers as appropriate.

GENERAL OBSERVATIONS AND DISCUSSION

Three themes emerge from our consideration of civic education advocacy: (1) a general reluctance of advocates to specify detailed assessment approaches; (2) concerns about prevailing assessment practices; and (3) disjunctures between professed civic education approaches and current approaches to assessment in general.

Reluctance to Specify Assessment

Many civic education advocates appear reluctant to talk in much detail regarding assessment and evaluation of what they are advocating. They are willing to outline the broad objectives of civic education in general or even the specific objectives of a particular program. To a lesser extent, advocates will talk of curriculum or learning activities or learning outcomes. But there is a reluctance to move from general goals to curriculum objectives to talk of assessment and evaluation. For the most part, when we do hear about assessment and evaluation of civic education, the talk is with a larger view, that is, national and international studies, comparisons across countries. Or the talk is with a considerably circumscribed view, with a discussion, say, of indices of tolerance. There is little said of assessment at the individual, classroom, and school levels.

What accounts for this silence? Perhaps some advocates are silent simply because they choose not to move to details. Surely we cannot expect every advocate to include an assessment discussion every time he or she speaks of civic education. Perhaps some feel reluctant to talk because they feel that assessment is not their area of expertise. Others perhaps do indeed have considerable expertise, and they know that to move from generalities to specifics about assessment is to move into an area of astonishing complexity; within the bounds of whatever document they are preparing, there simply is not room to address that complexity.

At the very least, we can observe that there is not a great deal of discussion and exchange regarding assessment, and very little of the give-and-take that should precede adoption of any major testing and evaluation initiative.

Concerns About Prevailing Assessment Practices

Although many civic education advocates appear reluctant to detail desired assessment designs, it will be noted that over the years other civic education advocates have expressed reservations about prevailing assessment practices. In 1934, the Commission on the Social Studies (American Historical Association, 1934) argued that civic education was "not susceptible of mathematical description" (p. 94). The Educational Policies Commission of 1940 cautioned that testing would drive the civic education curriculum and that "inappropriate" methods would limit or cripple civic education. In 1980, Remy expresses concern about the tendency of mass testing to trivialize citizenship and civic education. In 1999, Tolo argues that a focus on testing civic knowledge will lead to inadequate attention to participation skills and dispositions. In 2000, Kahne and coauthors warn that state-mandated testing in civic education leads to less likelihood of students engaging in higher order thinking or experiencing democracy as a way of life.

Civic Education and Assessment Disjunctures

There are three disjunctures to consider here. First, virtually all civic education advocates speak of some minimal combination of knowledge, skills, and dispositions necessary for a quality civic education program. But most current assessment practices focus on just one part—knowledge acquisition. Most people will agree that knowing, say, the First Amendment of the U.S. Constitution is important. And at one level of "knowledge of the First Amendment," that "knowledge" can be assessed. Identify correctly the five elements of the First Amendment, for example. We focus on this kind of "knowledge" or "learning" because it is, of course, cheap, the resultant data are easy to aggregate, and the test outcomes can be easily explained to school boards, parents, and reporters. Assessment of skills can be done, but at a higher price, much less efficiently, and with results that are more difficult to explain; most school districts and states are not willing to allocate significant resources to such assessment. As for dispositions, those habits of mind, or habits of the heart, these, too, can be assessed, but the costs are high and explanations to school boards, parents, and reporters quite complex, with various audiences asking just what is being measured with X tolerance scale, or with Y "portfolio," or Z "service" activity, and how does that relate to the program?

The second and third disjunctures stem from the common practice of focusing assessment and evaluation on individual student learning in the classroom.

Many civic education advocates argue that we have to measure more than student learning in the classroom. Many of these advocates will argue that a good civic education program must take place in a classroom that is democratically run, with the teacher not acting in authoritarian ways but in supportive, nondominant ways. If one accepts this argument, then one has to confront the contradiction posed by assessing and evaluating individual student learning. What learning there is must be considered part of a complex context, a network of relationships. If we as educators believe that there should be no contradictions between what we are teaching, how we are teaching, and how we are structuring our classrooms, and if we believe that there are such contradictions, then it is the extent of those very contradictions that need to be assessed, and not just knowledge acquisition.

The third disjuncture stems from the desire of many advocates to move the civic education action beyond the classroom. The classroom is important, to be sure, but it is just a part of the whole. It is the classroom plus the school, or it is the classroom plus the school plus the community that matters. We find as a common theme in the civic education literature the need for not only the classroom but the entire school to be democratically run, and for the school to be acting in concert with the community—its people and its several health, education, and welfare agencies—if we are to have a good civic education program. If one accepts the notion of moving beyond the classroom to the school, then assessment must necessarily focus in significant part on the conditions and circumstances of the school as an active center for civic education. Likewise, if one accepts the notion of acting in concert with the community in order to have a good civic education program, then assessment must focus in significant part on school–community circumstances and relations.

It is difficult to see how these three disjunctures can be dealt with effectively. But if these disjunctures cannot be resolved, then civic education is in a double bind. If civic education is to be a significant part of the curriculum and a significant part of what happens in the school, then civic education has to be part of the regular district and state assessment and evaluation program, part of what is going to be tested. This would appear to be a reasonable proposition, given what educators see every day as to its proof: What gets tested gets attention, what does not gets the crumbs or under-the-table attention. So to even be a part of any significant action, one has to buy into the mainline district- and state-level tests. But if civic education testing takes place at the district and state levels, that testing will in all likelihood focus on knowledge acquisition, with little attention paid to skills and dispositions. As such, what civic educators have to accept is a loss of what makes civic education valuable—the emphases not just on knowledge but on skills, dispositions, attitudes. Civic education advocates, then, are faced with a double bind. If they don't buy into district- and state-level testing, they lose. If they do buy in, they lose. And—the third part of a double-bind situation—they cannot choose not to play.

CONCLUDING COMMENTS AND RECOMMENDATIONS

Civic education advocates are in a difficult spot in determining how to respond to the demands for assessment of their endeavor. It appears that four response options are available.

First, as we have already noted, civic education advocates can refuse to join in the high-stakes assessment at the district or state (or, possibly, national) level. The disadvantage of the option is that civic education becomes marginalized and starved for resources: Only those subjects and areas being tested will be on the agenda.

Second, civic education advocates can participate in high-stakes assessment. The disadvantage is that civic education becomes trivialized with a narrow focus on knowledge acquisition—just one of many parts of a good civic education program.

Third, as an extension of the second option, advocates can in effect make a pact with the devil, acceding to high-stakes testing but on a sub-rosa basis, attending to the many other parts of a good civic education program as best as they can. This option appears to be popular; many advocates, recognizing that schools are loosely coupled organizations, continue to do what they deem necessary. The difficulty here is that advocates are not being direct in making their case for civic education.

There is a perennial struggle for resources, and there is ample opportunity for misunderstanding, with school boards, state education people, and the public continuing to view civic education in a narrow sense—the sense defined by the high-stakes tests—and advocates going in quite a different direction. The Machiavellian strategy of appearing to acquiesce while in fact subverting might be effective for a short period, but over time it will not provide a sound basis for civic education program advocacy.

The fourth option is the development of a conceptually solid, easily understandable means of assessing the kinds of civic education programs that most advocates have in mind, with a focus not just on knowledge acquisition and retention but on all of the other aspects of civic education as well—skills, attitudes, dispositions, "habits of the heart," and the like. To plump for this option will be difficult, as indicated by the silence we have noted on the part of many civic education advocates when faced with assessment challenges. But if these challenges can be met, if advocates can find persuasive yet nondemagogic ways of talking about their endeavors, then civic education can at last be put on a solid footing. It should not be necessary for all advocates to come to consensus as to program objectives and pedagogy. If one wants to make a case for heavy emphasis on an issues-oriented approach, then make the case and make the persuasive argument for the appropriate means of assessment, and likewise with a participation approach or any other way of framing a good civic education program.

The fourth option, then, would seem to be the most reasonable and ultimately the most persuasive option for civic education advocates.

If civic education is as central to school as is claimed, and if civic education is to be taken seriously, then we must have a responsible system of assessment and accountability based on all the complexities of civic education. If we do not choose to invest the attention and resources in such a responsible system, we must acknowledge that our claims for the centrality of civic education are just so many words not to be taken seriously.

NOTE

1. In Soder (2002), I provide more detail. Also useful for me have been Butts (1980, 1989), Hertzberg (1981), Parker (1996a, 1996b, 2001, 2002), and Shaver (1981).

REFERENCES

American Historical Association. Commission on the Social Studies in the Schools. (1934). *Conclusions and recommendations of the commission*. New York: Scribner's.

Battistoni, R. M. (1985). *Public schooling and the education of democratic citizens*. Jackson: University Press of Mississippi.

Boyte, H. (1994). Review of *Civitas:* A framework for civic education. *Teachers College Record, 95*(3), 414–418.

Brown, B. F. (Ed.). (1977). *Education for responsible citizenship: The report of the national task force on citizenship education*. New York: McGraw-Hill.

Butts, R. F. (1981). *The revival of civic learning: A rationale for citizenship education in American schools*. Bloomington, IN: Phi Delta Kappa Educational Foundation.

Butts, R. F. (1989). *The civic mission in educational reform: Perspectives for the public and the profession*. Stanford, CA: Hoover Institution Press.

Conover, P. J., & Searing, D. D. (2001). A political socialization perspective. In L. M. McDonnell, P. M. Timpane, & R. Benjamin (Eds.), *Rediscovering the democratic purposes of education* (pp. 91–124). Lawrence: University Press of Kansas.

Conrad, D., & Hedin, D. (1977a). Citizenship education through participation. In *Education for responsible citizenship: The report of the national task force on citizenship education* (pp. 133–155). New York: McGraw-Hill.

Conrad, D., & Hedin, D. (1977b). Learning and earning citizenship through participation. In J. P. Shaver (Ed.), *Building rationales for citizenship education* (pp. 48–73). Arlington, VA: National Council for Social Studies.

Cornbleth, C., Gay, G., & Dueck, K. G. (1981). Pluralism and unity. In H. D. Mehlinger & O. L. Davis, Jr. (Eds.), *The social studies: Eightieth yearbook of the National Society for the Study of Education* (pp. 170–189). Chicago: University of Chicago Press.

Diamond, S. E. (1953). *Schools and the development of good citizens: The final report of the citizenship education study*. Detroit, MI: Wayne University Press.

Dynneson, T. L., & Gross, R. E. (1991). The educational perspective: Citizenship education in American society. In R. E. Gross & T. L. Dynneson (Eds.), *Social science perspectives on citizenship education* (pp. 1–42). New York: Teachers College Press.

Educational Policies Commission. (1940). *Learning the ways of democracy: A case book of civic education*. Washington, DC: National Education Association and the American Association of School Administrators.

Ehman, L. H., & Hahn, C. L. (1981). Contributions of research to social studies education. In H. D. Mehlinger & O. L. Davis, Jr. (Eds.), *The social studies: Eightieth yearbook of the National Society for the Study of Education* (pp. 60–81). Chicago: University of Chicago Press.

Engle, S. H., & Ochoa, A. S. (1988). *Education for democratic citizenship: Decision making in the social sciences.* New York: Teachers College Press.

Gonzales, M. H., Riedel, E., Avery, P. G., & Sullivan, J. L. (2001). Rights and obligations in civic education: A content analysis of the *National Standards for Civics and Government. Theory and Research in Social Education, 29*(1), 109–128.

Hertzberg, H. W. (1981). *Social studies reform: 1880–1980.* Boulder, CO: Social Science Education Consortium.

Houser, N. O., & Kuzmic, J. J. (2001). Ethical citizenship in a postmodern world: Toward a more connected approach to social education for the twenty-first century. *Theory and Research in Social Education, 29*(3), 431–461.

Jones, T. J. (1913). *Statement of the chairman of the committee on social studies* (Bureau of Education Bulletin 1913, no. 41). Washington, DC: U.S. Government Printing Office.

Kahne, J., Rodriguez, M., Smith, B. A., & Thiede, K. (2000). Developing citizens for democracy? Assessing opportunities to learn in Chicago's social studies classrooms. *Theory and Research in Social Education, 28*(3), 311–338.

Kliebard, H. H. (1994). "That evil genius of the negro race": Thomas Jesse Jones and educational reform. *Journal of Curriculum and Supervision, 10*(1), 5–20.

Longstreet, W. S. (1985). Citizenship: The phantom core of social studies curriculum. *Theory and Practice in Social Education, 13*(2), 42–45.

Mehlinger, H. D. (1977). The crisis in civic education. In B. F. Brown (Ed.), *Education for responsible citizenship: The report of the national task force on citizenship education* (pp. 69–82). New York: McGraw-Hill.

Montesquieu, C. (1969). *De l'esprit des lois.* Paris: Garnier Freres. (Original work published 1750)

Morrissett, I. (1981). The needs of the future and the constraints of the past. In H. D. Mehlinger & O. L. Davis, Jr. (Eds.), *The social studies: Eightieth yearbook of the National Society for the Study of Education* (pp. 36–59). Chicago: University of Chicago Press.

Mosher, R., Kenny, R. A., Jr., & Garrod, A. (1994). *Preparing for citizenship: Teaching youth to live democratically.* Westport, CT: Praeger.

National Council for the Social Studies. (1997, April–May). Fostering civic virtue: Character education in the social studies. *Social Education,* 225–227.

Newmann, F. M. (1975). *Education for citizen action: Challenge for secondary curriculum.* Berkeley, CA: McCutchan.

Newmann, F. M. (1977a). Alternative approaches to citizenship education: A search for authenticity. In B. F. Brown (Ed.), *Education for responsible citizenship: The report of the national task force on citizenship education* (pp. 175–187). New York: McGraw-Hill.

Newmann, F. M. (1977b). Building a rationale for civic education. In J. P. Shaver (Ed.), *Building rationales for citizenship education* (pp. 1–33). Arlington, VA: National Council for Social Studies.

Pangle, T. L., & Pangle, L. S. (1993). *The learning of liberty: The educational ideas of the American founders.* Lawrence: University Press of Kansas.

Parker, W. C. (1996a). "Advanced" ideas about democracy: Toward a pluralist conception of citizen education. *Teachers College Record, 98*(1), 104–125.

Parker, W. C. (Ed.). (1996b). *Educating the democratic mind.* Albany: State University of New York Press.

Parker, W. C. (2001). Toward enlightened political engagement. In W. B. Stanley (Ed.), *Critical issues in social studies research* (pp. 97–118). Greenwich, CT: Information Age Press.

Parker, W. (Ed.). (2002). *Education for democracy: Contexts, curricula, assessments.* Greenwich, CT: Information Age Press.

Patrick, J. J., Vontz, T. S., & Nixon, W. A. (2002). Issue-centered education for democracy through Project Citizen. In W. Parker (Ed.), *Education for democracy: Contexts, curricula, assessments* (pp. 93–112). Greenwich, CT: Information Age Press.

Remy, R. (1980). *Handbook of basic citizenship competencies.* Arlington, VA: Association of Supervision and Curriculum Development.

Rose, L. C., & Gallup, A.M. (2000). The 32nd annual Phi Delta Kappa/Gallup Poll of the public's attitudes toward the public schools. *Phi Delta Kappan, 82*(1), 41–58.

Shaver, J. P. (1981). Citizenship, values, and morality in social studies. In H. D. Mehlinger & O. L. Davis, Jr. (Eds.), *The social studies: Eightieth yearbook of the National Society for the Study of Education* (pp. 105–125). Chicago: University of Chicago Press.

Soder, R. (2002). *Learning to be good citizens in a democracy: Reflections on assessment and evaluation practices in civic education (Occasional Paper No. 2).* Seattle: University of Washington, Institute for the Study of Educational Policy, Project PRAISE.

Tolo, K. W. (1999). *The civic education of American youth: From state policies to school district practices.* Austin: University of Texas, Lyndon B. Johnson School of Public Affairs.

Wehlage, G. G., Popkewitz, T. S., & Hartoonian, H. M. (1973, December). Social inquiry, schools, and state assessment. *Social Education,* 766–770.

Wexler, P., Grosshans, R. R., Zhang, Q. H., & Kim, B. (1991). The cultural perspective: Citizenship education in culture and society. In R. E. Gross & T.L. Dynneson (Eds.), *Social science perspectives on citizenship education* (pp. 141–160). New York: Teachers College Press.

CHAPTER 7

Strange, Yet Familiar: Assessment-Driven Education

Linda Mabry

"Make the familiar strange." With this memorable phrase, Fred Erickson (1986, p. 121) advised the qualitative researcher to treat common educational settings as exotic locales, to look into and beyond the ordinary, to understand underlying ideology, to see how values and assumptions shape reality. Those of us working in educational assessment and accountability need hardly trouble ourselves to make the familiar strange, for our familiar reality is already decidedly peculiar. The familiar phrase "test-driven curriculum," for example, denotes the bizarre idea that the proper role of assessment is to *monopolize* curriculum rather than to *monitor* what students have learned from it. No less jarring are the all-too-familiar phrases "test-driven educational reform" and "assessment-driven accountability." What could be stranger than the familiar advice to do "backwards planning" of instruction, beginning by identifying the student performances ultimately desired, as if students were not diverse, intentional beings who perform uniquely and unexpectedly? Why don't rubrics that specify in advance the criteria by which those unpredictable performances will be assessed seem strange? None of this seems strange, strangely. It has become familiar.

This chapter offers a perspective on concepts and practices familiar in measurement but little-known to critical stakeholders: educators, stu-

Holding Accountability Accountable. ISBN 0-8077-4464-6 (paper), ISBN 0-8077-4465-4 (cloth). Prior to photocopying items for classroom use, please contact the Copyright Clearance Center, Customer Service, 222 Rosewood Drive, Danvers, MA, 01923, USA, telephone (978) 750-8400.

dents, parents, society. Measurement shapes assessments and accountability policies that, in turn, shape education that, in turn, shapes society and the opportunities and lives of individuals. Momentous impact demands that measurement should be visible, available for public scrutiny, and open to debate and alternative interpretations. Instead measurement is obscure, accessible only to those schooled in its technical complexities, some of which are oddly inconsistent with educational theory and best practices — strange, because it is educational outcomes that are to be measured. The purpose of this text is to encourage reconsideration by those who are familiar with measurement strategies and awareness by those who are not, to encourage an informed estrangement from the familiar.

MUTUAL DISTRUST

Educational measurement arose from distrust of teachers. To avoid "the officious interference of the teacher," Horace Mann (1848) enacted the first standardized test in the United States, the 1846 Boston Survey, revoked in 1847, scores unused and scandalously low. A half-century later, Edward Thorndike (1921) in New York trumpeted a standardized alternative to teachers' grades, merely

> opinions rather than measurements, and subject to two notable defects. Nobody could be sure what was measured, or how closely the mark or grade tallied with the reality. . . . At least a million boys and girls, probably, were measured last year in respect to general intellectual capacity for school work. The number of such measures of reading, writing, spelling, arithmetic, history, and geography made during the year probably exceeded two millions. (pp. 372, 374)

Distrust of teachers remains a common theme:

> At AERA 2003, an Iowan defended traditional psychometrics, arguing that teachers do not assess student achievement as well as standardized tests do.
> "But wouldn't you agree, as most measurement experts do, that a teacher has a better evidentiary base for judgments of student achievement?" I asked him. "That, although there is measurement error in each grade on individual papers, that a teacher's overall inference of achievement is more likely to be valid than one based on a single test score?"
> "A better base, yes," he replied, "but I've been teaching measurement classes for thirty years, and I can tell you they make lots of mistakes in judg-

ing achievement. Unless they've taken a class like mine, a judgment based on a standardized test score is more likely to be valid." (April 21, 2003, session 22.071)

The word *assess* comes from Greek through old French, as Wiggins (1989) and Bracey (1998) note, meaning "to sit with." To understand a child's learning, a teacher sits with him or her. External test developers, high-stakes testing implementers, and, apparently, the Iowan do not. The intimacy of teacher appraisal and the remoteness of external testing found starkly contrasting views about student assessment.

Paradigmatic Conflict

The prevailing learning theory is *constructivism*, the idea that each person constructs his or her knowledge base, interpreting new information against prior knowledge, experience, values. This theory suggests attention to a student's background, goals, dispositions, and talents to recognize his or her achievement and, within the zone of *proximal development* (Vygotsky, 1978), to nudge him or her toward new discovery. Constructivist educators speak of individual differences, learning styles, multiple intelligences (Gardner, 1983); of students as active rather than passive learners; of themselves as facilitators or coaches (Wiggins, 1993).

Their practices reflect individualized, not one-size-fits-all, learning. Constructivist teachers *sit* with students and try to individualize assessment (Mabry, Poole, Redmond, & Schultz, 2003). They tend to favor John Dewey's (1909) "moral standard, by which to test the work of the school upon the side of what it does directly for individuals" (p. 53) over large-scale accountability. Teacher beliefs suggest a paradigm deeply at odds with that of standardized testing.

In standardized testing, the manifest theory is *behaviorism*, the idea that changed behavior, as an educational product, can be measured. Representing change on a numerical scale provides numbers, measurements, which can be statistically and psychometrically manipulated and plotted on a bell-shaped or normal curve. This is a different world from that of classrooms and comes with different ideas about what can be known of a student's achievement; it is a different paradigm.

Berlak and colleagues (1992) described the *psychometric paradigm*, its unmet assumptions and problems, and juxtaposed it against the *contextual paradigm* of classrooms. In standardized, norm-referenced testing—and even criterion-referenced tests exhibit norm-referenced characteristics (Bracey, 1998)—test content is curriculum-insensitive, treating each test-taker as if she or he enjoyed a learning opportunity equivalent to that of any other's. Regardless of individual differences and opportunities, test conditions must be identical to be considered fair. Contrastingly, in the contextual paradigm, students are tested with teacher-made instruments.over material actually presented to them What to teach and to test, when, and how are matters for teachers' professional judgments.

A tenet of an even more constructivist *personalized paradigm* (Mabry, 1999) is that understanding a personal knowledge base requires personalized assessment featuring individualized content, times, formats, and standards; sharing authority with students regarding content to be assessed and when and how; and taking into account each student's opportunities and goals. Here, treating test-takers as identical is unfair because of real differences among individuals, their backgrounds, and many other factors influencing achievement and performance.

The psychometric paradigm confers authority on persons far from classrooms, the contextual paradigm to practicing education professionals. The personalized paradigm offers joint authority to teachers and students, fostering development of students' personal responsibility. Strangely, it is the remote control of external assessments and accountability, not local openness (House, 1996), that are familiar and credible.

Political, Ethical, and Educational Implications

Mann (1848) envisioned education as "a great equalizer of the conditions of men, the balance wheel of the social machinery" and wanted measurement to help create an American meritocracy. But disparities between rich and poor, powerful and powerless, are increasing (Phillips, 2002). Teachers worry that testing is part of a political scheme favoring privatization and the wealthy at the expense of public education and the poor (Mabry, Aldarondo, & Daytner, 1999), less similar to Mann's than to Foucault's thinking about testing as

> surveillance that makes it possible to qualify, to classify, and to punish. . . . It manifests the subjection of those who are perceived as objects and the objectification of those who are subjected. (cited in Rabinow, 1984, p. 197)

As "the engine and odometer of reform," testing has been used

> to evaluate the competence of educators and the quality of educational systems, . . . to force restructuring, to control what is taught, to punish low-scoring students, to compel schools to comply with the mandates of policy-makers. (Mabry, 1999, p. 2)

For three decades, education has paid a heavy price to measurement:

- Narrowing of curricula to subjects, topics, and skills readily tested by multiple-choice items (Abrams, 2002; Smith, 1991; Wolf, 1993).
- Making curricula superficial and, in primary and pre-primary grades, inappropriately academic (Shepard & Smith, 1988).
- Reducing pedagogy to the teaching of "miscellaneous dead facts" (Meier, 1983; see also Bowman & Peng, 1972; Shepard & Dougherty, 1991).
- Diverting funds and instructional time to testing and test preparation (Madaus & Raczek, 1996; Smith, 1991).
- Demoralizing students (Berliner & Biddle, 1995; Smith, 1991).
- Deprofessionalizing teachers (Broadfoot, 1996; Jaeger, 1991; Smith, 1991).
- Misidentifying students and consequently misallocating educational resources because of test bias (Beckford & Cooley, 1993; Burton, 1996; College Board, 1990).
- Imposing high-stakes penalties on students such as retention, placements in low academic tracks, denial of graduation (Amrein & Berliner, 2002; Dorn, 2003; Haney, 2000; National Research Council, 2001).
- Imposing high-stakes penalties on teachers such as low evaluations, probation, firing (St. Louis Teachers Union v. St. Louis Board of Education, 1987).
- Imposing high-stakes penalties on schools such as public embarrassment and loss of autonomy (Bauer, 2000; Goertz & Duffy, 2001; Goodson & Foote, 2001; Meyer, Orlofsky, Skinner, & Spicer, 2002).
- Raising scores without raising achievement or "score pollution" (Haladyna, Nolen, & Haas, 1991).
- Reporting misleading information about student achievement and the quality of school programs (Cannell, 1987; Cooley & Bernauer, 1991; Gray, 1996; Linn, 2000), which encourages inappropriate educational policy and practices (McAllister, 1991; McLean, 1996; Shepard & Smith, 1988).
- Increasing the status of state assessment personnel over state curriculum personnel (Très-Brevig, 1993).
- Discouraging teachers and parents from staying with and helping to improve low-scoring schools (McLaughlin, 1991; Stein, 2000; Wilson & Corbett, 1989).
- Promoting parental loss of custody of children because of higher test scores in a competing spouse's school district (Colvin, 1997).

The history of standardized testing in education is one of good intentions — Binet's for humane education of disabled children, Mann's for fairness over privilege, Thorndike's for accuracy — but negative consequences have proven inevitable. Testing cannot eliminate measurement error and, with error, comes misguided policy and practice. A glimpse of the scale of these problems may be seen annually in reported scoring errors (*FairTest Examiner*, 1999a, 1999b; Galley, 2003; Grahnke, 1999). Universities recognize the superiority of grade-point averages (GPA) — teachers' grades — over test scores in determining student readiness for college (Cloud, 2001).

Recognizing measurement errors and the empirical superiority of GPAs should bring the argument full circle. If, after all, teachers' grades are superior, then the effort, expense, and notorious problems of standardized testing ought to be jettisoned. Instead, strangely, testing is a growth industry, familiar in schools and increasingly familiar in the media.

MEASUREMENT STRANGENESS

It is strange to refer to educational assessment as *measurement*, for constructs as elusive as achievement, intelligence, and aptitude cannot be confidently weighed on a bathroom scale or held against a yardstick. Assessing student achievement is a matter of inference. A student is asked to perform; from the performance, a judgment is made about its quality and an inference about what the student knows and can do. The inference is an estimate informed by the performance. No assignment of scores or calculation of standard errors of measurement — themselves estimates — changes the fact that assessment is about inferences.

Validity

Inferences and educational actions based on them must be valid — not tests or scores — if measurement is doing its job.

> Validity is an integrated evaluative judgment of the degree to which empirical evidence and theoretical rationales support the *adequacy* and *appropriateness* of *inferences* and *actions* based on test scores or other modes of assessment. (Messick, 1989, p. 13, emphasis in the original)

Validation. Strangely, *validation* of standardized tests does not involve consideration of the "*appropriateness* of *inferences* and *actions* based on test scores." It would be expensive to check what people think the scores mean or to see whether the actions triggered by scores are appropriate. Instead, validation typically involves examining (1) *content-related evidence* and (2) *criterion-related evidence of validity.* Content validation involves ensuring that test items have been "judged with high consensus to be relevant to the domain" (Messick, 1989, p. 37). But consensus, even among content experts, does not guarantee relevance.

Stranger yet, criterion-related validation involves correlating scores with scores from other tests of the same construct, such as math achievement, college readiness, academic giftedness. If Test A and Test B are both tests of college readiness, for example, the scores should positively correlate. SAT and ACT scores do, in fact, correlate positively. High SAT scorers overwhelmingly tend to be high ACT scorers and vice versa, evidence that the SAT and the ACT are tests of the same construct, as claimed. But a positive correlation would not show that Test A is a good test of the intended construct unless Test B was a good test of the intended construct. What is the evidence that Test B is a good test of the intended construct? Correlation with Test C, correlated with Test D, and so on. Psychometricians know these common practices, analogous to a hall of mirrors, are insufficient: "Granted, empirical test-criterion prediction alone often sustains test use in practice. But this is a strictly pragmatic basis, not necessarily a valid one" (Messick, 1989, p. 77). Surely, the public and educators should also know but they do not, and the measurement community is not making strong efforts to inform them.

Multiple measures. The best advice for promoting valid inferences of achievement is to use multiple measures — a variety of assessments, different types at different times, so that other assessments may compensate for the measurement error in each, all combining to produce a valid holistic inference of student achievement.

Multiple measures are common to classrooms but not to accountability testing,[1] where claims of school failure are based on no more than test scores in 12 states and where students can be denied promotion to the next grade on the basis of nothing more than test scores in five states or denied diplomas on the basis of nothing more than test scores in 19 states (Doherty & Skinner, 2003) — all in direct contradiction of:

- *The Standards for Educational and Psychological Testing* (AERA, APA, & NCME, 1999): *Standard 11.20.:* "In educational, clinical, and counseling settings, a test taker's score should not be interpreted in isolation; collateral information that may lead to alternative explanations for the examinee's test performance should be considered" (p. 117).

- The Standards for Educational Accountability Systems developed by the National Center for Research on Evaluation, Standards, and Student Testing (CRESST) and the Consortium for Policy Research in Education (CPRE) (Baker, Linn, Herman, & Koretz, 2002): "Decisions about individual students should not be made on the basis of a single test" (p. 3).
- The position statement of the National Association for the Education of Young Children (NAEYC, 1988): "Decisions that have a major impact on children such as enrollment, retention, or assignment to remedial or special classes should be based on multiple sources of information and should never be based on a single test score" (n.p.).

There are many such statements by professional organizations and states. Visitors to Washington state's assessment web site find acknowledgment of the importance of multiple measures (http://www.ospi. wednet.edu/; www.k12.wa.us) but, strangely, the state's plan is to base high school graduation in 2008 (for all but special education students) on nothing more than the Washington Assessment of Student Learning (WASL). Washington teachers know and do better (Mabry et al., 2003), but they are also held accountable on this thin basis as a result of recent federal legislation (Linn, Baker, & Betebenner, 2002; No Child Left Behind Act, 2001).

Reliability

In psychometrics, *reliability* means consistency — consistent scores on equivalent forms of the same test. Parents, educators, and policy makers would certainly want to know that a student's test score on one day was not a fluke — that she or he would get the same score, or very close to the same score, the next day, or the day after, or even the week after, a period of time where no major gain or loss in performance ability would be expected. To gauge empirically this kind of reliability, psychometricians would have to retest students on the same test or a parallel or equivalent test. If test-takers' scores varied considerably from one time to the next, the test would be unreliable and there would be little confidence in using the scores to grant entry to college or to deny diplomas.

It is expensive and time-consuming to administer tests two or more times, so cheaper methods are used. *Split-half* reliability is calculated from a single test with equivalent items such that two tests, in effect, are administered simultaneously. But it is expensive to offer twice the orindary number of items, so an even cheaper, but unfortunately not equivalent, procedure is used, *internal consistency*, and called "reliability."

Internal consistency. To avoid the expense of creating and administering parallel or long tests, developers assume that each *item* on the test is like a "test" in itself. Thus a 30-item test is treated as if it were 30 one-item tests. Items are intercorrelated to see how stable the scores are at the item level, and then, using mathematical formulae, stability at the total test level is estimated. The estimates are then passed off as "reliability" coefficients, although the stability of individual test score performance has not been investigated. Moreover, internal consistency coefficients are highly influenced by the number of items on the test, such that it is almost impossible *not* to obtain substantial internal consistency figures on most achievement tests provided the items are positively, but not necessarily highly, correlated.

Interrater reliability. For constructed-response or performance items, *interrater reliability* is sought — that is, consistent ratings by different raters scoring the same performance. In the Olympic Games, a familiar example, the highest and lowest scores by judges of diving and figure-skating are discarded because they are inconsistent (unreliable) in the context of the judging panel's scores.

But the unreliable highest or lowest score might actually be the best basis for inferring diving or skating quality; this is even more possible for student writing scored by poorly paid part-time corporation employees (Fortner, 2001; Hall, McDonald, Scherich, Vickers, & Zebrowski, 2001) who know nothing about the test-takers. Corporation scorers' reduced financial circumstances render them vulnerable to threats of firing if they do not score quickly and reliably enough (Vosburgh & Stephens, 2000), a situation more likely to promote conformity than deep thinking about performance and achievement.

Despite error-ridden past performance, corporations continue to win contracts to score many state high-stakes tests (Galley, 2003). State contracts specify scorer qualifications, minimum reliability, and deadlines. Scorer qualifications vary according to states' specifications, a few requiring a bachelor's degree in the subjects of the tests they score but, more commonly, 2 years of college suffices. Few corporation scorers are teachers, and scoring administrators prefer nonteachers and less well-educated scorers who offer fewer arguments about what a student's score should be (Mabry, 2001).

Stranger yet, states commonly require 70% to 80% reliability and sampling schemes where only 10% of student papers are read by two scorers. In such arrangements, which occur even for high-stakes tests, for every 100 papers scored, interrater reliability is determined for seven or eight and merely presumed for 92 to 93 (Mabry, 2001).

Even stranger, what counts as consistent is conveniently defined. Following the National Assessment of Educational Progress (NAEP) (http://nces.ed.gov/nationsreportcard) and the early Vermont writing rubrics (Vermont Department of Education, 1991), scoring rubrics commonly offer four performance levels as potential scores; the range among states is three to six performance levels (Mabry & Daytner, 1997). Having a small number of possible score levels has certain effects:

- Scores have less precision, just as there would be less precision in the grades of a teacher who awards only A-B-C-D grades than in the grades of a teacher who awards grades from A+ to F-.
- There are fewer score errors because there are fewer possibilities of errors, but those that occur, especially around the minimum "cut-score," are more serious (Yen, 1997).
- Interrater reliability is more likely, just as two teachers would be more likely to agree on a grade of A than to agree on the more specific A+, A, A-.

Vermont was aware that a constrained measurement scale would promote interrater reliability. Also to promote interrater reliability, the state determined that scorers need not select the same performance level in order to be considered scoring reliably; rather, "adjacent scores" would meet the state definition for reliability, also widely adopted by other states. The adjacent-scores definition of reliability resembles saying that an A from one teacher and a B from another are consistent. These two features of Vermont's much-imitated rubrics were admitted to be "rigging the system for reliability" (Brewer, 1991).

Manipulating reliability rather than monitoring levels of naturally occurring reliability is a strange development (Delandshere & Petrosky, 1998; Mabry, 1995; Moss, 1994), driven by a heightened sense of the importance of reliability given the difficulty and expense of determining validity.

Relationship Between Validity and Reliability

The measurement community universally regards validity as the most important principle in testing and, with almost equal frequency, considers reliability *necessary but not sufficient* for validity. The latter, strangely, is both true and false. True, reliability is *not sufficient* for validity: Consistency is not enough because consistent (reliable) scores can consistently promote invalid inferences. For example, consistent scores of zero on a multiple-choice science test written in English, earned each time they took the test, would have promoted the invalid inferences that Galilei Galileo, who was fluent in Italian, and Marie Curie, who was fluent in French, knew no science. Given a performance assessment instead, Galileo would have fared no better; his raters were the Inquisition, consistently wrong.

But it is false to claim that reliability is *necessary* for validity, as psychometricians and measurement textbooks do (e.g., Gronlund, 1993; Hopkins, Stanley, & Hopkins, 1990). Yes, it is hard to be sure that a test-taker who gets wildly different (unreliable) scores on the science test, or about whose performance judges greatly disagree, knows his or her science. But one of those scores might promote a valid inference of the test-taker's science achievement. It's just hard to know if one (or which one) does.

That the relationship between validity and reliability is discontinuous, parallel, is revealed in such cases as *Dalton v. Educational Testing Service* (1995). ETS claimed that Brian Dalton's higher, second SAT score was too inconsistent for release to colleges. Dalton sued on the basis that the second score was, in fact, valid; he won.

Consistency and consensus confer confidence that test-based inferences and actions are valid — but only confidence, not validity. The false assumption that reliability evidence is indirect validity evidence provides a theoretical basis for cheaper reliability efforts to be prioritized in practice. For testing corporations and nonprofit organizations such as ETS, which compete for state testing contracts (Bacon, 2001; Hoff, 2003), cheap counts.

A disturbing picture is formed by connecting the dots, as in Figure 7.1.

CONSEQUENTIAL VALIDITY

What matters in educational measurement is the validity of inferences based on scores, inferences manifest in actions that have consequences. Sam Messick's (1989) seminal articulation of validity theory spotlighted inferences and *consequential validity*:

Figure 7.1. How Test-driven Education Reform Results in Deformed Education.

The *intent* of assessment-driven accountability is reformed education. Its foundations:

1. *Validity* is critically important (i.e., whether test scores promote valid inferences and valid actions based on inferences).
   Comprehensive validation is expensive. Test corporations seek profits and avoid expense.
   Result: Inadequate validation is common.

2. *Reliability* (i.e., consistent scores) is less important than validity.
   Reliability is considered necessary for validity. With validity evidence inadequate, reliability evidence, cheaper to obtain, gains importance.
   Result: Reliability is prioritized over validity in practice.
   Measures of internal consistency, called "reliability coefficients," are cheaper to obtain than measures of reliability.
   Result: Reliability is not calculated. Internal consistency is substituted for reliability.
   Few understand how "reliability" is defined and practiced.
   Result: They typically accept test corporation claims and legal defenses.
   Standardization promotes consistency.
   Result: Assessment-driven accountability involves standardized tests, standardized test administration, standardized scorer training, standardized rubrics, and standards specifying test content and performance.

3. *High-stakes* consequences are typically based on tests with weak validity evidence and questionable reliability evidence. Stakes are high enough to make teaching to the test inevitable.

The *unintended consequence* of assessment-driven accountability is *de-formed* education.

What is to be validated is not the test or observation device as such but the inferences derived from test scores of other indicators — inferences about score meaning or interpretation and about the *implications for action* that the interpretation entails. (p. 13, emphasis added)

Consequences in the Standards

The next-to-last draft of the *Standards for Educational and Psychological Testing* (AERA, 1999) defined validity much as Messick (1989) did (see earlier) but ultimately downplayed consequential validity:

Validity refers to the degree to which evidence and theory support the interpretations of test scores entailed by *proposed* uses of tests. (p. 9, emphasis added)

Although information about the consequences of testing may influence decisions about test use, such consequences do not in and of themselves detract from the validity of *intended* test interpretations. (p. 16, emphasis added)

The *Standards* thus announce that, in psychometrics, intentions matter more than consequences, and children and educators can expect the measurement community to mount no defense on their behalf. The *Standards* free the measurement community from using its expertise to shield education from inappropriate consequences of testing.

Measurement experts accepting state consulting contracts have a vested interest in test-driven accountability. States are increasingly dependent on them and test corporations as staffs are cut (Mabry & Daytner, 1997) and hired away by test corporations. There is little public recognition of these relationships and few admonitions against them other than the following unenforceable public statement by the American Evaluation Association (2002):

Test publishers should publicly object and refuse future contracts with users when the publishers' tests are misused. . . . Measurement specialists and advisors involved in high stakes testing programs [should] consider not only technical and theoretical but also consequential issues, such as the welfare of students, educators, schools, and society. . . . Contractors for testing services, state or local, should demand appropriate validation studies.

Consequences in Real Settings

Like the *Standards,* Messick (1989) argued that the existence of negative test consequences was not a technical issue:

It is not that adverse social consequences render test use invalid but, rather, that the validation of test use should assure that the adverse social consequences do not stem from any source of test invalidity, such as construct-irrelevant variance. (p. 68)

I argue, however, that "adverse social consequences," whether or not they "stem from any source of test invalidity," should be considered in validation. Because it is impossible to construct a test free from measurement error, and impossible to identify all sources and impacts of measurement error in a test, it is impossible to determine unequivocally whether the measurement error in a test contributes to "adverse social consequences." Only in the psychometric paradigm can error-free testing or identifying all sources and impacts of measurement error be imagined.

Messick (1989) understood that this theoretical world doesn't exist and that exceptions are always needed:

> There is, indeed, a good rationale for why sound professional judgment should have veto power in practice: otherwise [the 1985 *Standards for Educational and Psychological Testing*] would be completely prescriptive and, hence, unresponsive to compelling local exceptions. (p. 91)

His argument for putting "sound professional judgment" ahead of external testing "unresponsive to compelling local exceptions" acknowledges the uniqueness of local educational needs. Messick also recognized the difficulty of achieving equity:

> At this point, it appears difficult if not impossible to be fair to individuals in terms of equity, to groups in terms of parity or the avoidance of adverse impact, to institutions in terms of efficiency, and to society in terms of benefits and risks — all at the same time. . . . In practice, . . . balancing of needs and values almost always comes down to a political resolution. (p. 78)

The pervasiveness of familiar inequities in education, which test-driven accountability confirms and promotes in awarding high scores to the nurtured and low scores to the neglected, cries out for educator "veto power" and "political resolution," unlike familiar state and national testing policies. With few exceptions,[2] current policies prefer questionable psychometric assumptions and practices and, increasingly and especially in the latest federal incursion into state testing practices (No Child Left Behind Act of 2001), demand unrealistic educational change.

Teachers do not object to being held accountable but to unreasonable accountability (Abrams, 2002). Psychometricians and the teachers whose "quality" is impugned by NCLB understand why the law's goals are unrealistic and its punishments unfair to the students who must struggle hardest and who, ironically, are most likely to be left behind. But federal officials seem not to have asked professionals in either education or measurement what might actually constitute appropriate educational assessment and accountability. Strange.

NOTES

1. Spurious arguments are currently being proffered that different parts of a test or retakes of the same test satisfy the testing standards requirement that high-stakes decisions be based on multiple measures.

2. Exception: Nebraska is attempting to maintain local control of assessments used for accountability purposes in the face of NCLB pressure (Roschewski, Christensen, & Buckendahl, 2001).

REFERENCES

Abrams, L. (2002, April). *Multi-state analysis of the effects of state-mandated testing programs on teaching and learning: Results of the national survey of teachers.* Paper presented at the annual meeting of the American Educational Research Association, New Orleans, LA.

American Educational Research Association (AERA), American Psychological Association (APA), & National Council on Measurement in Education (NCME). (1999). *Standards for educational and psychological testing.* Washington, DC: AERA.

American Educational Research Association. (2003). Annual Meeting, Session 22.071, "Making assessments constructive: large-scale and classroom."

American Evaluation Association (AEA). (2002). Task Force on High Stakes Testing (L. Mabry, S. Mathison, J. Sanders, R. E. Stake, D. Stufflebeam, & C. Thomas). Position statement on high stakes testing in preK–12 education. Fairhaven, MA: AEA. Available from http://www.eval.org

Amrein, A. L., & Berliner, D. C. (2002). High-stakes testing, uncertainty, and student learning. *Education Policy Analysis Archives, 10*(18), 1–63.

Bacon, D. (2000, April 16). School testing: An education-industrial complex is emerging. *Oakland Tribune,* distributed online by *Common Dreams Newscenter,* http://www.commondreams.org/views/041600-109.htm.

Baker, E. L., Linn, R. L., Herman, J. L., & Koretz, D. (2002, Winter). Standards for educational accountability systems. *CRESST Line,* 1–4.

Bauer, S. C. (2000). Should achievement tests be used to judge school quality? *Education Policy Analysis Archives, 8*(46), 1–19.

Beckford, I. A. & Cooley, W. W. (1993, December). The racial achievement gap in Pennsylvania. *Pennsylvania Educational Policy Studies, 18.*

Berlak, H., Newmann, F. M., Adams, E., Archbald, D. A., Burgess, T., Raven, J., & Romberg, T. A. (1992). *Toward a new science of educational testing and assessment.* Albany: State University of New York Press.

Berliner, D. C., & Biddle, B. J. (1995). *The manufactured crisis: Myths, fraud, and the attack on America's public schools.* Reading, MA: Addison-Wesley.

Bowman, C. M., & Peng, S. S. (1972). *A preliminary investigation of recent advanced psychology tests from the GRE program – An application of a cognitive classification system.* unpublished ETS report, Princeton, NJ.

Bracey, G. W. (1998). *Put to the test: An educator's and consumer's guide to standardized testing.* Bloomington, IN: Phi Delta Kappa.

Brewer, R. (1991, June). *Portfolio assessment — Findings from research and practice.* Presentation to the Alternative Assessment Conference of the Education Commission of the States and the Colorado Department of Education, Breckenridge, CO.

Broadfoot, P. (Ed.). (1986). *Profiles and records of achievement: A review of issues and practice.* London: Cassell Education.

Burton, N. (1996). Have changes in the SAT affected women's mathematics performance? *Educational Measurement: Issues and Practice, 15*(4), 5–9.

Cannell, J. J. (1987). Nationally normed elementary achievement testing in America's public schools: How all 50 states are above the national average. *Educational Measurement: Issues and Practice, 7*(2), 5–9.

Cloud, J. (2001, March 12). Should SATs matter? *TIME,* 62–67, 70.

The College Board. (1990). *College bound seniors national report, 1990.* New York: Author.

Colvin, R. L. (1997, December 31). Can essay tests really make the grade? *Los Angeles Times, Valley Edition,* pp. A1, 24–25.

Cooley, W. W., & Bernauer, J. A. (1991). *School comparisons in statewide testing programs* (Pennsylvania Educational Policy Studies, Paper No. 3). Pittsburgh, PA: Pittsburgh University School of Education, Learning and Development Center.

Delandshere, G., & Petrosky, A. R. (1998). Assessment of complex performances: Limitations of key measurement assumptions. *Educational Researcher, 27*(2), 14-24.

Dewey, J. (1909). *Moral principles in education.* Carbondale: Southern Illinois University Press.

Doherty, K. M., & Skinner, R. A. (2003, January 9). State of the states. In *Quality counts 2003: If I can't learn from you . . .* (a report on education in the 50 states by the Editorial Projects in Education). *Education Week, 22*(17), 75–105.

Dorn, S. (2003). High-stakes testing and the history of graduation. *Education Policy Analysis Archives, 11*(1), 1–28.

Erickson, F. (1986). Qualitative methods in research on teaching. In M. C. Wittrock (Ed.), *Handbook of research on teaching* (3rd ed., pp. 119–161). New York: Macmillan.

FairTest Examiner. (1999a, Fall). No safety in numbers. Available from http://www.fairtest.org/examarts/fall99/No_Safety_in_Numbers.html

FairTest Examiner. (1999b, Winter). Test-scoring error. Available from http://www.fairtest.org/examarts/winter99/examind.html

Fortner, C. (2001, September 18). Who's scoring those high-stakes tests? Poorly trained temps. *Christian Science Monitor,* http://www.csmonitor.com/2001/0918/p19s1-lekt.html

Galley, M. (2003, June 18). More errors are seen in the scoring of tests, Boston researchers say. *Education Week, 22*(41), 10.

Gardner, H. (1983). *Frames of mind: The theory of multiple intelligences.* New York: Basic Books.

Goertz, M. E., & Duffy, M. C. (with LeFloch, K. C.). (2001, March). *Assessment and accountability systems in the fifty states: 1999-2000. CPRE Research Report Series RR-046.* Philadelphia: University of Pennsylvania Graduate School of Education, Consortium for Policy Research in Education.

Goodson, I., & Foote, M. (2001). Testing times: A school case study. *Education Policy Analysis Archives, 9*(2), 1–10.

Grahnke, L. (1998, August 17). Part-time workers score achievement essay tests: Temps making the grade—for others. *Chicago Sun-Times.* Available from: http://web.lexis-nexis.com/universe

Gray, J. (1996). The use of assessment to compare institutions. In H. Goldstein & T. Lewis (Eds.), *Assessment: Problems, developments and statistical issues* (pp. 121-133). New York: John Wiley & Sons.

Gronlund, N. E. (1993). *How to make achievement tests and assessments* (5th ed.). Boston: Allyn & Bacon.

Haladyna, T. M., Nolen, S. B., & Haas, N. S. (1991). Raising standardized achievement test scores and the origins of test score pollution. *Educational Researcher, 20*(5), 2–7.

Hall, B., McDonald, J., Scherich, H., Vickers, D., & Zebrowski, M. (2001, June). *Performance scoring—The challenges and opportunities in today's assessment world.* Panel presentation to the CCSSO Large-Scale Assessment Conference, Houston, TX.

Haney, W. (2000). The myth of the Texas miracle in education. *Education Policy Analysis Archives, 8* (41).

Hoff, D. J. (2003, May 28). Nonprofit ETS making quick surge into K–12 market. *Education Week, 22*(38), 8.

Hopkins, K. D., Stanley, J. C., & Hopkins, B. R. (1990). *Educational and psychological measurement and evaluation.* Boston: Allyn & Bacon.

House, E. R. (1996). A framework for appraising educational reforms. *Educational Researcher, 25*(7), 6–14.

Jaeger, R. M. (1991). Legislative perspectives on statewide testing. *Phi Delta Kappan, 73*(3), 239–242.

Linn, R. L. (2000). Assessments and accountability. *Educational Researcher, 29*(2), 4-16.

Linn, R. L., Baker, E. L., & Betebenner, D. W. (2002). Accountability systems: Implications of requirements of the No Child Left Behind Act of 2001. *Educational Researcher, 31*(6), 3–16.

Mabry, L. (1995, April). *Naturally occurring reliability.* Paper presented at the annual meeting of the American Educational Research Association, San Francisco, CA.

Mabry, L. (1999). *Portfolios plus: A critical guide to alternative assessments and portfolios.* Thousand Oaks, CA: Corwin Press.

Mabry, L. (2001, March). *Issues in scoring state-mandated performance assessment.* Presentation to the National Academy of Education-Spencer Foundation, Palo Alto, CA.

Mabry, L., Aldarondo, J., & Daytner, K. (1999). *Local administration of state-man-*

dated performance assessments: Implications for validity. Paper presented at the annual meeting of the American Educational Research Association, Montreal, Quebec, Canada.

Mabry, L., & Daytner, K. G. (1997, March). *State-mandated performance assessment.* Paper presented at the annual meeting of the American Educational Research Association, Chicago, IL.

Mabry, L., Poole, J., Redmond, L., & Schultz, A. (2003, April). Local impact of state-mandated testing. *Education Policy Analysis Archives, 11*(22).

Madaus, G. F., & Raczek, A. E. (1996). The extent and growth of educational testing in the United States: 1956–1994. In H. Goldstein & T. Lewis (Eds.), *Assessment: Problems, developments and statistical issues* (pp. 145–165). New York: John Wiley & Sons.

Mann, H. (1848). Available from http://www.tncrimlaw.com/civil_bible/horace_mann.htm

McAllister, P. H. (1991). Overview of state legislation to regulate standardized testing. *Educational Measurement: Issues and Practice, 10*(4), 19–22.

McLaughlin, M. S. (1991). Test-based accountability as a reform strategy. *Phi Delta Kappan, 73*(3), 248–252.

McLean, L. D. (1996). Large-scale assessment programmes in different countries and international comparisons. In H. Goldstein & T. Lewis (Eds.), *Assessment: Problems, developments and statistical issues* (pp. 189–207). New York: John Wiley & Sons.

Meier, D. (1983). "Getting tough" in the schools: A critique of the conservative prescription. *Dissent,* 61-70.

Messick, S. (1989). Validity. In R. L. Linn (Ed.), *Educational measurement* (3rd ed., pp. 13-103). New York: American Council on Education, Macmillan.

Meyer, L., Orlofsky, G. F., Skinner, R. A., & Spicer, S. (2002). The state of the states. In *Quality counts 2002: Building blocks for success* (a report on education in the 50 states by the Editorial Projects in Education). *Education Week, 21*(17), 68–92.

Moss, P. A. (1994). Can there be validity without reliability? *Educational Researcher, 23*(2), 5–12.

National Association for the Education of Young Children. (1988). NAEYC position statement on standardized testing of young children 3 through 8 years of age, adopted November 1987. *Young Children, 43*(3), 42–47.

National Research Council. (2001). Chapter 4: Effects of high-stakes testing and standards. In *Understanding dropouts: Statistics, strategies, and high-stakes testing.* Washington, DC: National Academies Press.

No Child Left Behind Act of 2001, Pub. L. No. 107–110th Cong., Rec. 1425. 115 Stat. (2002).

Peter Dalton v. Educational Testing Service. (1995). 87 NY wd 384, 633 N.E. 2d 289, 639 N.Y.S. 2d 977.

Phillips, K. (2002). *Wealth and democracy: A political history of the American rich.* New York: Broadway Books.

Rabinow, P. (Ed.). (1984). *The Foucault reader.* New York: Pantheon.

Roschewski, P., Christensen, D., & Buckendahl, C. (2001, June). *Standards, assessment, and accountability – A balanced approach.* Presentation to the CCSSO Large-Scale Assessment Conference, Houston, TX.

Shepard, L. A., & Dougherty, K. C. (1991, April). *Effects of high stakes testing on instruction.* Paper presented at the annual meeting of the American Educational Research Association, Chicago, IL.

Shepard, L. A., & Smith, M. L. (1988). Escalating academic demand in kindergarten: Counterproductive policies. *Elementary School Journal, 89*(2), 135–145.

Smith, M. L. (1991). Put to the test: The effects of external testing on teachers. *Educational Researcher, 20*(5), 8–11.

Stein, S. J. (2000). Opportunity to learn as a policy outcome measure. *Studies in Educational Evaluation, 26*(4), 289–314.

St. Louis Teachers Union v. St. Louis Board of Education, 652 F. Supp. 425 [37 Ed. Law Rep. [798]] (E.D. Mo. 1987).

Thorndike, E. L. (1921). Measurement in education. *Teachers' College Record, 22*(5), 371–397.

Très-Brevig, M. da P. (1993). *Effects of implementation of assessment policy on staff practices at a state department of education.* Unpublished doctoral dissertation, University of Illinois at Urbana-Champaign.

Vermont Department of Education. (1991). *Vermont's assessment program.* Montpelier: Author.

Vosburgh, M., & Stephens, S. (2000, February 25). Temps grade crucial student tests: Part-time workers check 30-35 exams an hour. *Plain Dealer.* Available from: http://web.lexis-nexis.com/universe

Vygotsky, L. S. (1978). *Mind in society: The development of higher mental process.* Cambridge, MA: Harvard University Press.

Wiggins, G. (1989). A true test: Toward more authentic and equitable assessment. *Phi Delta Kappan, 70*(9), 703–713.

Wiggins, G. (1993). *Assessing student performance.* San Francisco: Jossey-Bass.

Wilson, B. L., & Corbett, D. (1989). *Two state minimum competency testing programs and their effects on curriculum and instruction.* Philadelphia: Research for Better Schools.

Wolf, A. (1993). *Assessment issues and problems in a criterion-based system.* London: Further Education Unit.

Yen, W. M. (1997, March). *Measuring school performance: Is "percent of students reaching standards" the most accurate statistic?* Paper presented at the annual meeting of the American Educational Research Association, Chicago, IL.

CHAPTER 8

Responsible Accountability and Teacher Learning

Patricia A. Wasley

The movement to create high standards for all children, coupled with high-stakes measurements, has dominated this country's educational agenda for the past decade. High-stakes tests are being implemented state by state, and the emerging results have led to a shift in the debate. In one state after another, the results are showing that children from advantaged backgrounds are doing reasonably well, whereas poor children, many of them children of color, are not achieving at the rate many had hoped. Naturally, parents and policy makers are asking why. Are the nation's schools so bad that they can't get kids ready for a test? Should we abandon public education because it doesn't seem to be working? Are teachers just lazy or unwilling to make the necessary effort? And with the current federal mandate to "leave no child behind," educators are feeling pressured to either produce results or suffer the consequences: state takeovers of local districts, sanctions for individual schools, charter legislation, vouchers.

The unfortunate part of this sequence of events is that it was and still is remarkably predictable. Although everyone agrees that putting standards in place has been important, merely setting standards is not enough. To believe so is like believing that a high jumper can exceed his or her best record just by raising the bar to a higher level. Or that all we need to do to be less dependent on fossil fuels is to create an electric car

Holding Accountability Accountable. ISBN 0-8077-4464-6 (paper), ISBN 0-8077-4465-4 (cloth). Prior to photocopying items for classroom use, please contact the Copyright Clearance Center, Customer Service, 222 Rosewood Drive, Danvers, MA, 01923, USA, telephone (978) 750-8400.

(which was accomplished in the 1800s!) (Schiffer, Butts, & Grimm, 1994). Unfortunately, higher achievement is never that simple for athletes, for the auto industry, or for children in public schools.

In order to explain why setting high standards and instituting high-stakes tests has not enabled poor children to meet the standards, I wish to examine multiple dimensions of teachers' work: First, teachers' responsibilities have changed substantially in the course of the last 20 years. Second, conditions that support teachers' professional growth have not kept pace with changes in their responsibilities. In order to build a truly responsible accountability system, support for and our investment in ongoing teacher growth must be commensurate with our investment in both standards and ways to assess student accomplishment.

CHANGING PERCEPTIONS, CHANGING RESPONSIBILITIES

As reported by the National Center for Education Statistics, the United States has some 3.4 million elementary and secondary teachers. In the middle of the last century, an enormous effort was made to "scientize" education, which meant that many of the leading educators were seeking scientific explanations to explain learning and to organize schools (Ravitch, 2000). Their work slowly convinced educators and policy makers that there is a normal distribution of learning as represented by the familiar bell curve. Many of the teachers currently in the public schools were taught to look for this distribution of achievement, and by inference, of intelligence. Common practice and belief held that in any given class, the quartile system of dividing up the normal curve should be an empirical reality — one fourth of the students would achieve well below the average, one half of the group would be in the average range, and the remaining fourth would be well above average. In courses in colleges and universities across the country, teachers were taught to distribute grades in this way. It was not that teachers were taught to believe that particular children were stupid or that labeling children before assessing their work was acceptable. Instead, the underlying assumption, and often the belief, was that, for any given group of children, a predictable proportion of children would do well while a predictable proportion would not. The corresponding belief was that teachers' primary responsibilities were to deliver the curriculum — what children should know — and then figure out what the distribution of learning was. Although most teachers worked hard to ensure that their students were successful, many grew to believe that poor children and children of color do not achieve as well as their more privileged White counterparts because they saw these differences play out in their own classrooms. It is also true that teachers teach the way they were taught themselves (Lortie, 1975). As students, many teachers were taught by teachers who did not believe that all children could learn. The bell curve, then, became a kind of self-fulfilling prophecy influencing teachers around the country for decades.

The irony here is rich. Whereas thousands upon thousands of teachers were taught that the normal distribution was appropriate, few encountered disconfirming evidence like *The Mismeasure of Man,* a book written over 20 years ago, describing how intelligence testing was developed by the Armed Forces in order to prove differential intelligence based on race (Gould, 1981).

It is only recently that we have begun to challenge the application of the bell curve to classroom achievement. New developments in cognitive sciences, neurological sciences, and studies on cultural differences, as well as the influence of the civil rights movement and pressures from big business to create schools that are globally competitive—all of these developments have come together to change our theories of learning. Vivid examples of poor children demonstrating remarkable achievement have emerged from unexpected places all across the country; and this, too, has convinced educators that poor kids can achieve high standards (see Freedman, 1990; Meier, 1995; Suskind, 1998). New teachers are now taught that every child can learn, provided that the teachers take advantage of the child's prior knowledge and adapt instruction to his or her cultural background and/or pedagogical dispositions (Bransford, Brown, & Cocking, 2000). The key to being successful with a diverse group of children is that teachers must have the variety of approaches, the depth of subject-matter knowledge, and the diagnostic skills to determine and facilitate what each child needs. And they must do all of this within educational systems that have not changed the nature of their professional support, the structure of the working day, or in most cases the number of children with whom they must succeed.

Not so long ago, while the dean at the Bank Street College of Education, I had the opportunity to teach two afternoons a week in the School for Children, located within the college. I had a room full of 26 very bright fifth and sixth graders. They varied enormously. Leslie was an artist; Shoshana a writer; Mojique a sometimes bully and a math whiz. Some were exceptional at reading. Others were good at science, while still others excelled only once a week when we had music. Several were very boisterous, whereas another small group of boys were quiet but always finding ways to play computer games without my noticing. Some listened to oral reading with rapt attention, while others went immediately to sleep. In many cases, I was able to locate their strengths. Because they were always present all together, I was not always able to find the individual time needed to figure out how to work on the weaknesses of every child. With some, sure; but not with all. When I noticed something that was stumping a large group of them, we would stop to learn about it. I believed I was reasonably successful, but everyone did not achieve at an equal level.

Simply developing the systems for keeping track of kids' work in two disciplines was a major undertaking. Then making sure that I understood the subject matter well enough to field the many directions in which kids want to go was hard. Further, analyzing their work to understand why they got the answers they did, or structured sentences the ways they did, was enormously time consuming. I used to time it: Each paper took me 20 to 30 minutes in order to give each child the feedback he or she needed to feel encouraged and challenged to learn more about whatever they were doing wrong. Times 26. Just writing. Their regular teacher had to teach everything: math, science, reading, literature, social studies, and then figure out how to use computers to enhance learning in any one of these subjects. And plan for each of these 5 days a week. To do this well, to ensure that all kids meet high standards, is really a killer job.

Every teacher faces the same kind of challenges each year. Kids just simply differ one from the other. In part that is what makes teaching so much fun, like a rolling mystery, so intellectually stimulating. In recent years, however, with greater press for teachers to ensure that every child succeeds by meeting high standards, teachers often feel overwhelmed and undersupported. And they are! Teachers are deeply aware that although a substantial investment has been made at the state and federal level to set standards and to develop high-stakes tests, little has been invested to help them develop the skills they need to meet these new, more complex responsibilities. Across the country, we have behaved as if we believed that mechanics who worked on biplanes could simply switch to jets without new training, or that we need only to set the bar higher to get the pole-vaulter to compete at higher levels. It has been a tremendously frustrating and demoralizing experience for teachers who know very well that getting every child in their class to achieve at much higher levels requires a good deal more than a set of standards and a single assessment. The scope of these new responsibilities suggests that enormous changes are needed in a teacher's system of support.

TEACHER QUALITY AND STUDENT ACCOMPLISHMENT

It is important to note that there is plenty of research that links student achievement to a highly qualified teacher. The National Commission on Teaching and America's Future (NCTAF) has reviewed the literature on the relationship between student accomplishment and qualified teachers. Its 1996 report, *What Matters Most: Teaching and America's Future*, states that

> studies show that teacher expertise is the most important factor in student achievement. A recent study of more than 1,000 school districts concluded that every additional dollar spent on more highly qualified teachers netted greater improvements in student achievement than did any other use of school resources. Another study, comparing high-achieving and low-achieving elementary schools with similar student characteristics, found that differences in teacher qualifications accounted for more than 90% of the variation in student achievement in reading and mathematics. (p.8)

Many districts across the country are using value-added assessment, a new system of tracking the relationship between teacher quality and student achievement. Sanders and Rivers (1996) provide evidence suggesting that a qualified teacher every year is essential to student accomplishment. Their data show the negative effects of having a poorly prepared teacher year after year; the cumulative loss in achievement gains for children is devastating.

This research then leads us to examine what it means to be a highly qualified teacher. What kinds of skills do highly qualified teachers have, and how do they learn what they need to know? What kind of support is needed?

HIGHLY QUALIFIED TEACHERS

Currently, a number of states are working to define what it means to be a highly qualified teacher. Again, the NCTAF (1996) suggests that

> expert teachers use knowledge about children and their learning to fashion lessons that connect ideas to students' experiences. They create a wide vari-

ety of learning opportunities that make subject matter come alive for young people who learn in very different ways. They know how to support students' continuing development and motivation to achieve while creating incremental steps that help students progress toward more complicated ideas and performances. They know how to diagnose sources of problems in students' learning and how to identify strengths on which to build. These skills make the difference between teaching that creates learning and teaching that just marks time. (p. 9)

Research colleagues and I conducted a study that led us to believe that having a significant repertoire in each of the four areas in a teacher's purview—curriculum, pedagogy, assessment, and school structure—makes an enormous difference in student engagement and learning (Wasley, Hampel, & Clark, 1996). We followed 150 students through their high school experiences. When teachers organize highly routinized classes, children figure out the routines almost immediately; then, given the predictability of the class, they determine how to get away with minimal performance. For instance, if their math class follows a predictable pattern of reviewing the homework from the night before, learning a new dimension of a math solution, and then doing homework for the next day, students learn to split the number of homework problems among themselves, or each student in a small group takes responsibility for a particular day, and so forth. In this way they limit their engagement and oftentimes their understanding of the subject matter. We could identify similar patterns in nearly all disciplines: in English, read a book, have a discussion, write a paper; or in science, read the chapter, discuss vocabulary, do a lab activity like the one the teacher has modeled, take a test. Whenever I describe these common instructional patterns and the corresponding strategies that students use to cope, people of all ages chuckle. Most of us used the same coping strategies when we were kids, and we use them now in our own work situations with predictable routines!

The confounding part of this situation is that many teachers are unaware of the effects of routine classes. They believe that they have a richly diverse approach to teaching. For them, variation is embedded in curricular genres or topics. For instance, a high school English teacher moves among poems, short stories, novels, plays. To an adult who has chosen the discipline, this variation is significant, rich, and compelling. For adolescents, this is not always the case.

In every school that we studied, however, and in every discipline, we found certain teachers who understood the needs of their students and appropriately varied their approach to the discipline as well as to the curricular content. A language teacher used up to eight different activities in each class period: sentence construction, recitation, conjugation, conversation about something significant, and so on. She used buzzers, egg-timers, bells placed around the room to signal a switch to a new activity, and she constantly moved around the room. Kids sat forward in their desks concentrating so that they could keep up with her. They loved the class and oftentimes said they felt exhausted from it – in a good way.

An English teacher had a very different approach to variation. She started her class at the beginning of the year by having them read a book, participate in a discussion, then write a paper. Next, she engaged students in web-based inquiry to develop a good definition of poetry. That was followed by an interdisciplinary unit she did with the social studies teacher. And she conducted Socratic seminars to read the Articles of Confederation. Because she varied the curricular content, the pedagogy, and the assessments, kids stayed with her. Parents jockeyed to get their kids into the classes of these teachers where students felt the most stimulated.

In order to teach like this, teachers need a significant repertoire of approaches. And such a repertoire requires constant professional growth, in the same way that actors or musicians need to continue to add pieces to their repertoires. These teachers described their professional work life as deeply engaging, intellectually stimulating, and as a source of constant study. The English teacher stated that she concentrated on learning how to teach various components of the writing process over a period of 5 years, mastering one component each year. She focused on learning how to do Socratic seminars with another colleague for nearly 3 years before she felt she fully understood its purpose and was confident in her ability to use it with her students. To learn to apply each new approach as more than a superficial activity and to understand the corresponding assessments, she needed outside experts or courses to demonstrate and allow her to apply the technique. Then she needed the time to find the materials she would use that would fit into her own curriculum. Further, she needed a colleague who could watch her while she was using the technique, then give her feedback; and she also needed feedback from her students. Going to a course offered outside of her school did not enable her to transfer what she had learned. Using the technique once in her own setting was simply insufficient to master the complexity of the strategy, and practicing alone did not provide her with enough feedback to grasp all the elements and nuances of the approach.

Research done by another group of scholars indicates that pedagogical content knowledge is critical if students are to truly understand a particular discipline. Grossman (1990) suggests that a teacher must be familiar with four dimensions of teaching any particular content:

- Knowledge and beliefs about teaching a particular subject at a variety of grade levels.
- Knowledge of students' understandings and misunderstandings about a particular discipline.
- Knowledge of curricular materials available.
- Knowledge of particular strategies for teaching and representing particular content.

These dimensions of subject-matter knowledge are not covered in an undergraduate degree, because the emphasis is on covering the domain rather than concentrating on how to teach it. Again, even highly qualified teachers need time to master each of these dimensions of the disciplines they teach.

Wineburg (2001), in his book *Historical Thinking and Other Unnatural Acts*, explores what it really takes to teach history. Clearly, most of us have forgotten the list of dates and names that we were once required to memorize. Also, clearly, it is important that we actually know the significance of some dates, names, and places in order to integrate historical knowledge into our daily contexts. More important, however, is the need to understand the context of the time, the back-and-forthing of the various players inherent in any historically significant event. It is these things that bring history to life and enable us to analyze the similarities and differences between an earlier time and our own (Wineburg, 2001).

Naturally, we want teachers to have a deep and complex understanding of their disciplines. Such understanding takes time and effort to cultivate. Teachers need to work on each of these dimensions, and they need to work on them over time, so that their understandings of children and subject matter become more sophisticated (Grossman, 1990).

PROFESSIONAL CONTEXT AND TEACHER LEARNING

A great deal of research has been conducted on teacher learning and the effects of typical school contexts. Some of the earliest and most consistent findings suggest that conditions in schools miligate against teacher learning:

1. Teachers work in isolation.
2. They get little meaningful feedback on their work.
3. They are exposed to little data on how their children are doing other than their own classroom assessments.
4. Teachers work in an egalitarian culture that makes it difficult to engage in mutual critique.
5. Induction into the profession is unsupported.
6. Elementary teachers have too many subjects and need legitimate expertise in all of them to teach them well.
7. High school teachers have too many students to know them well or to give them real feedback on their work.
8. Parents are frequently not provided meaningful roles in the school or treated as partners by teachers (Lortie,1975; Goodlad, 1984; Sizer, 1984; Waller, 1961; Wasley, 1991).

Most of these conditions persist today making it difficult for teachers to learn consistently and conscientiously.

Further research on the context of teaching reveals the seriousness of an unsupported entry into the profession: Schools have distinct adult-learning cultures that are not always supportive of new teachers. Because of this, far too many teachers leave the profession within the first 5 years. The Project on the Next Generation of Teachers at Harvard describes the conditions as follows:

> The questions and uncertainty that new teachers bring to school require far more than orientation meetings, a mentor in the building, directions to the supply closet and a written copy of the school's discipline policy. What new teachers want in their induction is experienced colleagues who will take their daily dilemmas seriously, watch them teach and provide feedback, help them develop instructional strategies, model skilled teaching and share insights about students' work and lives. (Johnson & Kardos, 2003, p. 13)

Little and McLaughlin (1993) found that when school learning communities were focused on the norms of collaboration as opposed to the norms of privacy, they worked together to examine children's work, deepen their understanding of subject matter, and figure out how to approach the curricular materials they had to work with. In these collaborative cultures, teachers were more satisfied and more confident in their abilities to help students.

Professional cultures exist in a number of forms. McLaughlin and Talbert (2001) describe departments and grade levels as teachers' primary affiliations and how these strengthen a teacher when focused on inquiry and collaborative learning. Lieberman and Miller (2001) document how teacher networks like those that have emerged around the National Writing Project or the Foxfire Outreach Networks engage teachers in sustained investigations.

In another study of teachers' work life, Grossman, Wineburg, & Woolworth (2000) discovered that oftentimes, teachers participate in "pseudo communities." That is, they do not feel free to critique each other's ideas, or challenge their understanding of subject matter, because the strong norms of privacy and politeness mitigate against such activity. The authors make the case that in order for teachers to have a vibrant intellectual life inside of schools, they have to have time for sustained engagement; and they need external mediators and expertise to guide them toward deeply intellectual work.

In order for teachers to "leave no child behind," they need time to learn on the job, they need data that give them information about what they need to do differently with the children they are working with. And they need expert support and time to work with their colleagues. These recommendations are clearly articulated in the *National Staff Development Council's Standards for Professional Development* (2003). These standards deal with context, process, and content standards; and, in all cases, standards are designed to improve the learning of all students. Some school districts such as Seattle have invested substantially in the development of their own professional growth standards. Every standard is supported by knowledge of content, prerequisite relationships, content-related pedagogy, inquiry and exploration, technology, the age group of the children, and a variety of strategies and accommodations (Seattle Public Schools, 2001). These standards make the case that teachers' growth is central to children's accomplishment.

Unfortunately, such staff development is still rare.

SUPPORT FOR STAFF DEVELOPMENT

Two dimensions of staff development practices are problematic when considering teachers' abilities to be responsible for all the children they teach. First, many school districts persist in offering professional development that involves one-shot, quick-fix workshops without appropriate connection to the issues individual teachers face with their students, or without site-based support or sustained inquiry to make real professional growth possible. Oftentimes, professional development opportunities are planned without any reference to the children actually served by teachers. Although it has been clear for some time that such work has been proven unlikely to change teaching, these forms still persist.

The second dimension is naturally related to the first. School districts nationwide spend a very small proportion of their budgets on staff development. In a 2001 survey conducted by the National Staff Development Council, 18% of respondents spent less than 1% of their overall budget on staff development, whereas 51% spent between 1% and 5%. Twenty-seven percent of those responding spent 6% to 10%, whereas only about 5% of the responding districts spent more than 10%.

By contrast, *Training* magazine's "Industry 2001 Report" states that "businesses are still investing billions of dollars annually in the hopes of capitalizing on the one true competitive advantage: human capital" (Galvin, 2001, p. 1). This same report notes that in 2001, U.S. organizations were expected to spend $56.8 billion on training. For example, some 25% of Microsoft's overall budget is spent on training, according to information provided recently by corporate representatives. Professional development resources at Microsoft are allocated to work groups to use as they see fit in order to tackle a new objective or to gain the skills needed to develop a new solution.

No major industry in the country would consider spending as little as education does to support the developing capacity of its employees. Moreover, for private industry, training is also a critical retention tool: "Substantial training investments engender a brand of loyalty that bears little resemblance to the job-for-life mentality of yesteryear" (Krell, 2002, p. 54). Smart employees want to know that the company will support their continued development; and they count this as a critical consideration in their employment package. IBM reported that it spent $1 billion annually on employee training using a variety of methods (Bolch, 2001). Companies that invest in their employees invest in their continued improvement and in their growth; and they retain their employees and their investments in them.

It is clear that although expectations of teachers and their responsibilities have changed substantially, the necessary investment to allow them to learn the new skills and approaches that would enable them to be successful with all students have not been forthcoming. Were investments in teacher development growing proportionally as part of the increasing standards movement, we would have a much less predictable problem facing us today.

CONCLUSIONS

To ensure that teachers are truly enabled to take full responsibility for their students' achievement, we first need to provide them with evidence that the old bell curve is no longer defensible, and we need to help them understand the dimensions of new responsibilities to help every child succeed. Nationwide, even greater financial resources than have gone to setting standards and to developing tests are really necessary to address the next part of the equation: teacher growth. Students need high-quality teachers. In order to become high-quality teachers, current educators need the capacity to develop a sophisticated, intellectually rigorous repertoire of approaches that are grounded in the subject matter, and that are appropriate for the children they teach. Further, they need professional development that provides for novice, mid-career, and experienced teachers.No matter how long teachers have been teaching, they need to continue to build their skills and knowledge.

My colleagues in Seattle describe appropriate professional support as context-based, ongoing, and site-specific. The context in which teachers teach must change substantially: a reduction in isolation, supported entry, concentration on inquiry into their own teaching, and the development of collaborative learning communities. Teachers need all of these things. To support such conditions and the ongoing development of their capacity, they need budget allocations that are greater than what we spend on testing each year. This would demonstrate the seriousness with which the federal government, states, and local school districts regard their responsibilities to ensure that teachers can be responsibly accountable for the learning of the children they serve.

REFERENCES

Bolch, M. (2001). IBM. *Training, 38*(3), 76–77.

Bransford, J.D., Brown, A.L., & Cocking, R.R.(Eds.). (2000). *How people learn: Brain, mind, experience, and school*. Commission on Behavioral and Social Sciences and Education, National Research Council. Washington, DC: National Academy Press.

Freedman, S.G. (1990). *Small victories: The real world of a teacher, her students, and their high school*. New York: Harper & Row.

Galvin, T. (2001). Industry 2001 report. *Training, 38*(10), 1–12.

Goodlad, J.I. (1984). *A place called school: Prospects for the future*. New York: McGraw-Hill.

Gould, S.J.(1981). *The mismeasure of man*. New York: Norton.

Grossman, P.L. (1990). *The making of a teacher: Teacher knowledge and teacher education*. New York: Teachers College Press.

Grossman, P., Wineburg, S., & Woolworth, S. (2000). *What makes teacher community different from a gathering of teachers?* Occasional paper cosponsored by the Center for the Study of Teaching and Policy and Center on English

Learning & Achievement. Seattle: University of Washington.

Johnson, S.M., & Kardos, S.M. (2002). Keeping new teachers in mind. *Educational Leadership, 59*(6), 12–16.

Krell, E. (2001). Greener pastures. *Training, 38*(11), 54–59.

Lieberman, A., & Miller, L.(Eds.). (2001). *Teachers caught in the action: Professional development that matters.* New York: Teachers College Press.

Little, J., & McLaughlin, M.W. (1993). *Teachers work: Individuals, colleagues, and contexts.* New York: Teachers College Press.

Lortie, D.C. (1975). *Schoolteacher: A sociological study.* Chicago: University of Chicago Press.

McLaughlin, M.W., & Talbert, J.E. (2001). *Professional communities and the work of high school teaching.* Chicago: University of Chicago Press.

Meier, D. (1995). *The power of their ideas: Lessons for America from a small school in Harlem.* Boston: Beacon Press.

National Commission on Teaching and America's Future. (1996). *What matters most: Teaching for America's future.* New York: Author.

National Staff Development Council. (2003). *NSDC standards for staff development.* Retrieved April 4, 2003, from http://www.nsdc.org/educatorindex.htm.

Ravitch, D. (2000). *Left back: A century of battles over school reform.* New York: Simon and Schuster.

Sanders, W.L., & Rivers, J.C. (1996). *Cumulative and residual effects of teachers on future student academic achievement.* Knoxville: University of Tennessee, Value-added Research and Assessment Center.

Schiffer, M.B., Butts, T.C., & Grimm, K.K. (1994). *Taking charge: The electric automobile in America.* Washington, DC: Smithsonian Institution Press.

Seattle Public Schools. (2001). *Professional practice standards: A guide to world-class teaching and learning.* Seattle, WA: Author.

Sizer, T.R. (1984). *Horace's compromise.* Boston: Houghton Mifflin.

Suskind, R. (1998). *A hope in the unseen: An American odyssey from the inner city to the Ivy League.* New York: Broadway Books.

Waller, W. (1961). *The sociology of teaching.* New York: Russell & Russell.

Wasley, P.A. (1991). *Teachers who lead: The rhetoric of reform and the realities of practice.* New York: Teachers College Press.

Wasley, P.A., Hampel, R.L., & Clark, R.W. (1997). *Kids and school reform.* San Francisco: Jossey-Bass.

Wineburg, S. (2001). *Historical thinking and other unnatural acts.* Philadelphia: Temple University Press.

Holding Accountability Accountable— Hope for the Future?

Kenneth A. Sirotnik

If one airplane in every four crashed between takeoff and landing, people would refuse to fly. If one automobile in every four went out of control and caused a fatal accident or permanent injury, Detroit would be closed down tomorrow.

Our schools—which produce a more important product than airplanes or automobiles—somehow fail one youngster in four. And so far we have not succeeded in preventing the social and economic fatalities every school dropout represents. . . .

However, thanks to a set of recent developments, so far little noted, we can now sharply cut this waste of lives and money. In fact, American educators now have an opportunity so far-reaching that . . .*we can transform our schools within this decade.*

This opportunity springs from . . . a new and sophisticated process of management that defines educational goals in measurable terms; from stimulating innovations discovered by new alliances among local schools, the federal government, and private enterprise; from testing programs that can be used at low political, social, and economic risk to discover what actually works; from the ability to avoid bureaucratic delay and put effective programs in the classrooms immediately; and from the growing acceptance of the idea that the schools, like other sectors of our society, are accountable to the public for what they do—or fail to do. (Lessinger, 1970, p. 3)

So begins a text that is remarkably contemporary were it not for a bit of late 1960s- or early 1970s-sounding lingo. Indeed the title of the book is *Every Kid a Winner,* a rhetorically identical but positive version of a more contemporary document, *No Child Left Behind* (2001). In the former, Leon Lessinger puts forward in 1970 a position statement reflecting an ideology of educational accountability that pretty much holds sway to the present day.[1]

HOLDING ACCOUNTABILITY ACCOUNTABLE

One form of accountability or another has always been present in American public schooling. But as Cuban shows us in Chapter 1, conceptions changed significantly in the wake of major federal legislation in 1965 (the Elementary and Secondary Education Act). Shifting from older, input-oriented models of accountability (e.g., measurable school resources) to an output-oriented model (e.g., measurable student performance), Lessinger (the Associate U.S. Commissioner of Education from 1968 to 1970) constructed his accountability argument on several still-familiar grounds.

First, he argued that it was irresponsible to continue the poor education of the nation's inner-city students, and that student performance is what counts.

> Performance statistics in the inner-city schools reveal that many children . . . are prepared for nothing but another generation of failure. For the well-being of our society, we cannot afford to perpetuate this parody of education. Many parents, disturbed by years of vague talk for the schools, are demanding performance, not more promises. (Lessinger, 1970, p. 4)

Second, Lessinger assumed that schools could, indeed, be places where all students could learn, and teachers, indeed, could make this happen. The problem, he believed, was with how the schools were organized and the paradigms guiding their practices.

> If schools are to be held accountable for results, they must develop a new approach to their basic mission. . . . They must define their output no longer as teaching done, but as learning proven. . . . What we need is data for all children that shows the educational gain produced by specific sequences of teaching. (p. 9)

Finally, Lessinger's silver bullet for the needed paradigmatic change was "a process of educational engineering. ... Everybody knows that in engineering we define exactly what we want, then bring together resources and technology in such a way as to assure those results" (pp. 12-13). And for Lessinger, those "results" were clear and measurable:

> When a program in the schools is well engineered, it will . . . require educational planners to specify, in measurable terms, what they are trying to accomplish. It will provide for an independent audit of results. . . .Above all, it will guarantee results in terms of what the students can actually do. (p. 13)

In turn, this accountability argument (including worries about the least-well-served students and the promise of measurable outcomes) formed the centerpiece of Nixon's educational address in 1970, when he tells the nation about "another new concept—*accountability*. School administrators and school teachers alike are responsible for their performance, and it is in their interest, as well as in the interests of their pupils, that they be held accountable" (cited in Glass, 1972, p. 637).

Does any of this sound familiar? Well, you might not find the "social engineering" type of lingo being used these days, and Lessinger's and Nixon's concerns focused mainly on basic skills, triggering the minimum-competency types of assessment and accountability to follow. Yet in a fundamental respect—the logic of the argument—little has changed in terms of the problem or the solution in over three decades.

For example (and exercising great restraint in not reviewing essentially the same ideology in the 1994 Goals 2000 rhetoric), let's consider the basic rationale in the 2001 No Child Left Behind (NCLB) Act (the reauthorization of the 1965 Elementary and Secondary Education Act). In President Bush's foreword to the report, we find sentiments remarkably similar to those expressed by Lessinger and Nixon: "Too many children in America are segregated by low expectations, illiteracy, and self-doubt. . . . It doesn't have to be that way."

And if it doesn't have to be this way, then what way should it be? The answer is the NCLB (2001) rationale as expressed in this "blueprint":

> *Increased Accountability for Student Performance.* . . . Achievement will be rewarded. Failure will be sanctioned. . . .*Focus on What Works.* . . . Federal dollars will be spent on effective, research based programs and practices. . . . *Reduce Bureaucracy and Increase Flexibility.* . . . *Empower Parents.* . . . Students in persistently low-performing schools will be given choice. (p. 2, emphasis in the original)

Thus, although current talk among some policy makers, politicians, and even educators (both researchers and practitioners) suggests the sudden recognition of the "achievement gap" and a "new era" of accountability as represented in NCLB, I would argue that this talk differs little from the rhetoric of 1970s. Both are outcome-driven (whether "standards-" or "objectives-based"); both rely on reward and punishment as motivational drivers; both assume that "Science" can prevail (whether cast as "social engineering" or "research-based practice"); and both lament the low achievement of economically poor children and many children of color. The only thing new about the "achievement gap" is the phrase.

I submit that as a nation we have had over three contemporary decades to make this kind of logic work for school improvement and change. Yes, the current rhetoric emphasizes "high standards" (vs. "minimum competency"); yet, wouldn't we have expected an easier task in shooting for minimum competency instead of "world class standards"? And for those who argue that it is only with NCLB that we finally have real teeth in school-level accountability policy, I argue that these teeth are false and the policy is disingenuous when, among other things, it provides nothing resembling the magnitude of resources necessary to turn around our most troubled schools.

No, contrary to claims that a new day has dawned in public school accountability concepts and practices, I argue that we continue mostly in the dark ages of old accountabilist arguments that have failed to deliver in any significant and lasting way.

It is also worth noting that critiques of accountability in the 1970s (e.g., Glass, 1972; Popkewitz & Wehlage, 1973; *Theory Into Practice*, 1979) are just as relevant today as they were then. As noted in my introduction to this volume, one of the more compelling critiques was that of Martin, Overholt, and Urban (1975). Their account of what they termed the "accountabilist" paradigm should be quite familiar:

> The notion that all or most of educational objectives should be couched in behavioral terms, the requirement that pedagogy be competence- or performance-based, the insistence on a strategy of educational evaluation which limits itself to that which can be observed and measured, and a call for the use of techniques of behavioral control which depend on an assumed instrumental relationship between means . . . and ends. (p. 3)

Following historical, educational, economic, and political critiques, these authors came to an interesting conclusion:

> Our examination of the accountability movement has led us to conclude that it is not an educational but rather political movement fueled by economic concerns. Economic and political forces provide the main thrust behind the movement that has attracted many who really believe that it will improve education. These forces aim to hold down costs at all levels of education while at the same time striving to maintain the economic and political status quo, complete with all its present inequities. (Martin et al., p. 75)

One is left with the overwhelming urge to say, "The more things change, the more they remain the same." This aphorism might even be a source of some comfort if it were not for the predictable and deleterious fallout of accountabilist theory and practice—fallout that continues to plague disproportionately those very students about whom accountabilists profess concern. This hypocrisy is palpable in an accountabilist rhetoric that screams out for equalizing student outcomes yet is conspicuously silent on the extraordinary inequities in a still racist and classist society within which we still try to conduct the great American experiment of public schooling (Goodlad, 1985).

I have previewed many of these concerns in the Introduction, and much has been elaborated upon by the contributors to this volume. Perhaps the most generous read of traditional accountability is Cuban's reflection in Chapter 1 on the history of the phenomenon and his suggested yes–no answers to the question, "Has outcome-driven (post-1965-style) accountability improved schooling?"

Cuban's "no" answers are straightforward and echo perennial concerns: narrowed focus of the function of schooling to measurable goals in academic basics; exclusion of alternative types of viable schools (e.g., progressive, community-based); faith in the ever-attractive but false theory of school-focused incentives and penalties to effect systemic change when it is clear that underachievement is a far more complex phenomenon (structurally, socially, politically, and economically); and, deemphasis of more in-depth performance assessment methods as well as methods based on teacher judgment and reflective practice.

Interestingly, Cuban's "yes" answers are all accompanied by caveats, each signaling (to me, anyway) far greater costs than benefits. To the benefit of coalition-building between schools, communities, and business over past years of sustained talk of school reform and accountability is added the potential cost of narrowing the broad goals of public schooling in a political and social democracy. To the benefit of focusing and sustaining attention on equity are added the potential costs of reifying the "achievement gap" and actually believing that equity obtains when test scores are equalized (see also the discussion in Chapter 4 by

Noguera). To the benefit of shifting focus from inputs to measurable outcomes is added the potential for ignoring some of the most critical (but not easily or cheaply measured) purposes of public schooling, for example, preparation for civic engagement in a democratic society (see also Soder's discussion in Chapter 6). To the above negatives, I would also add the obvious loss of focusing, in fact, *on inputs,* which remains critical to any hope of realizing equity and excellence in schools (see the discussion in Chapter 5 by Oakes, Blasi, and Rogers).

Finally, Cuban suggests that standards-based accountability has forced policy makers to realize the critical connection between teaching and learning, between building the capacity of educators and increased student performance. Yet, as Cuban points out, even if policy makers have come to this rather obvious realization, it is paradoxical in light of a core feature of traditional accountability arguments, namely, that it is teachers' lack of resolve, not ability, that leads to poor student achievement. Coupled with the huge investment of resources required to actually tackle needed capacity-building (see Wasley's discussion in Chapter 8), it is little wonder such efforts are, as Cuban notes, "splintered and erratic."

Cuban's "no" answers, therefore, stand on their own. And his "yes" answers all require highly consequential, negative caveats. On the whole, in my view, this does not make for a particularly stellar history of accountability in public education. In Chapter 2, Nancy Beadie takes another important route through the history of accountability and focuses attention on the moral consequences of traditional accountability theory and practice, particularly in terms of how it plays out for students. Through her historical analysis that traces roots back to the 19th century, she reveals the very real tensions between setting standards, on the one hand, and doing little or nothing to deal with preexisting inequities, on the other.

Ultimately and typically, those who end up benefiting most from social reforms in education tend to be children who need them least (Goodlad, 1984).

HOPE FOR THE FUTURE

The primary purpose and bulk of this book has been to critique traditional accountability concepts and practices. As such, this book is one in a long line of similar efforts, for as long as we have had accountabilist ideologies attempting to control public education, we have heard the critical voices of educators deconstructing these ideologies. We are certainly part of this latter chorus, and I hope we have added some fresh perspectives and new insights.

I suppose, also, that by virtue of the same critique here of traditional accountability — its record of longevity and failure — so goes the record of those, like us, who continue our own critiques. Perhaps the only comfort is in staying the course and maintaining the dialectic.

But perhaps not. Perhaps part of the failure to overcome the lure of traditional accountability practices is the failure to offer truly viable alternatives — not that some haven't tried (e.g., Berlak et al., 1992). The hard fact of the matter, however, is that there are no easy alternatives. Part of the attractiveness of the accountabilist ideology is its simplicity and reductionism: consequences (high stakes), easy to obtain evidence (testing), behavioralizing outcomes (or standards and performance, if you prefer), and laying the whole of the responsibility on the doorsteps of schools as if they existed in a social, political, and economic vacuum.

Nonetheless, until the educational community (P–12 through higher education) finds persuasive alternatives to account for what goes on in public schooling, we are likely stuck in this cycle of accountabilism, predictable fallout, and predictable critique.

Where, then, do we go from here? In this book, and through our critiques, my colleagues and I have suggested alternative beliefs and knowledge-based ideas that could form an alternative perspective — "responsibilism," I suppose. This perspective is rooted in beliefs more consistent with a more just and equitable democratic society and political system, with what we know about good teaching and learning, and with the educational needs of students and their families, particularly in economically poor communities and in communities of color.[2]

Beliefs

First, *public education must play a vital role in our pluralistic and democratic society.* The very survival of a political democracy depends on a participating, educated, and critically minded citizenry (Barber, 1993; Gutmann, 1987; Parker, 2003; Soder, 2001; and see also Siegel, Chapter 3, and Soder, Chapter 6, this volume). Our public education system must therefore guarantee an equitable and empowering education for all the nation's children and youth, and our federal, state, and local policies must support and nurture the schools in this effort by helping to create and sustain the conditions and circumstances within which the guarantee can be realized (Noguera, Chapter 4, this volume).

Second, *the functions of public education must be construed broadly to encompass the character and competencies of fully educated human beings, capable of filling multiple roles in our social and political democracy.* Although schools must attend to career opportunities for all students, solely utilitarian or economic narratives should not control the purposes of schooling (Siegel, Chapter 3, this volume). There is no better preparation for the future than preparing for lifelong learning in the present.

Third, *government and the public have a right to know how well children are faring in our public education systems.* To be accountable, according to the *American Heritage College Dictionary*, is to be "liable to being called into account; answerable." Those who are responsible for educating our children, therefore, must be called into account by parents, communities, the state, and perhaps even the nation—*assuming these constituent groups are willing to support what is necessary for appropriate and responsible educational conditions and practices.*

Thus, fourth, *just as educators need to be held accountable, so do policy makers and the public as a whole for the validity of the educational accountability systems they establish and the social and political conditions within which they expect these systems to work.* A society that is still marked by substantial racism and classism cannot expect just and equitable public schools no matter how much imploring about better leadership, better teaching, and "closing the achievement gap" (Oakes, Blasi, & Rogers, Chapter 5, this volume). Schools and society are inexorably bound together, as they should be. Improving both requires the will and work to make both better.

Fifth, *the distribution of resources in response to school- and community-based needs is not a fiscally or morally neutral event.* Taking a moral stance will require the courage to operate on the principle that "equal is not necessarily equitable," and that substantially more resources will have to be distributed to the least advantaged schools and communities (Rawls, 1971).

Finally, *accountability and responsibility must go hand in hand.* Responsibility includes accountability but also includes more layered meanings centered on being "able to make moral or rational decisions," being "trustworthy or dependable or reliable," and "showing good judgment." To be both *responsible and accountable* demands that we care deeply about the well-being of our children and that we bring the best ideas, the best knowledge, and the best practices and professional judgments to bear on the education of future citizens of our society and our world (Mabry, Chapter 7, this volume).

These beliefs, and others like them, can form a foundation upon which to build more responsible practices for "calling into account" ourselves as a social and political democracy, the political infrastructure supporting public schooling, and the system of schooling itself. But we also need to make use of what we know about good educational practices.

Good Educational Practices

All knowledge is tentative and contextual; nonetheless, we are not without many insights in education based on research, experience, and conceptual inquiry and critique.

First, other than for reasons of economy and efficiency, there is no educational justification for using on-demand, easily scored tests — and only those tests — to make high-stakes decisions about the educational well-being of children and their schools. No modern organization would ever use a single indicator to judge the worth of its operation — the GNP for the federal government or the average temperature of patients in a hospital, for example. No sensible hospital director would mandate more frequent temperature taking to cure patients; and no governmental body would endorse more frequent computation of the GDP to improve the economy. Yet we find ourselves, again, in an era where mandating more and more testing of students is expected to result in better teaching and learning. A responsible accountability system will abandon, once and for all, this accountabilist ideology.

Second, good assessment is a natural part of good teaching and learning (Mabry, Chapter 7, this volume; Shepard, 2000), it takes time, and it is not cheap. A responsible accountability system will be classroom-based (Taylor & Nolen, 2004) and will include the professional judgment of educators (Wheelock, 1998) and multiple indicators and assessments, quantitative and qualitative, over extended periods of time, that are sensitive to the needs of each individual student.

Third, a democratic nation's vitality — the ability of its citizens to participate thoughtfully and responsibly — is obviously threatened by a narrowly educated public. Test-driven, high-stakes accountability systems inevitably narrow what gets emphasized and how it gets emphasized in school curricula (Shepard, 1991; see also Siegel, Chapter 3, and Soder, Chapter 6, this volume). A responsible accountability system must include ways to assess all the valued goal areas (academic, social, personal, and career) of a comprehensive public education in forms consistent with what we know about children and their developmental processes.

Fourth, individual differences are critically important and children develop differently and have different styles of learning (Corno & Snow, 1986; Gardner, 1991; Gay, 2000). A "one size fits all" policy of teaching, learning, assessment, and accountability makes no sense and is doomed to failure. Retention policies don't work (Shepard & Smith, 1989) and serve only to increase dropout rates and diminish the economic and social well-being of our society (Catterall, 1987; Rumberger, 2001). A responsible accountability system will accommodate and promote ways of powerfully addressing the developmental needs of the individuals these systems are obligated to serve (Mabry, Chapter 7, this volume).

Fifth, students need extensive, high-quality opportunities to learn. This is about as obvious as it gets when it comes to pedagogical principles. The older time-on-task and academic learning time research (e.g., Berliner, 1979; Rosenshine, 1979) certainly supports this, as does the more recent research that takes a more complex look at conceptualizing opportunity to learn (e.g., The Leigh Burstein Legacy, 1995). As argued by Oakes, Blasi, and Rogers in Chapter 5, many schools — particularly those with high concentrations of children of poverty and children of color — are far too underresourced to do the job reasonably well. Prevailing conditions such as tracking and large school and class sizes further contribute to the decline of opportunities to learn (Finn & Achilles, 1990; Meier, 1995). A responsible accountability system must find ways to negotiate and assess the very difficult but critical balance between (1) the constraints of deplorable conditions and circumstances within which many public schools and educators try to do their work and (2) notwithstanding these constraints, the moral responsibility to do their work anyway — with the care and stewardship required for a quality education for all students.

Sixth, better teaching produces better results (Brophy & Good, 1986; National Commission on Teaching and America's Future, 1996). However, the magnitude of resources required for ongoing professional development of teachers — consistent with new developments in the disciplines and higher expectations for teaching, learning, and assessment — is huge compared to the minuscule amounts in current educational budgets (Wasley, Chapter 8, this volume). Responsibility in an accountability system will be demonstrated by substantial and continual opportunities for teachers and administrators to develop and improve their leadership and teaching capabilities.

Seventh, punishment and/or the threat of punishment are not productive ways to change behavior, either for individuals or for groups

(Baldwin & Baldwin, 1998; Sidman, 1989). Policy makers, however, continue to believe (or at least promote the notion) that the only way to improve teaching and learning is to have the threat of sanctions in accountability systems—real "teeth" that have biting consequences, for example, linking high school graduation to passing standards-based examinations. Otherwise, they argue, teachers won't take reform seriously, nor will their students.

Beadie's analysis in Chapter 2 suggests that this reasoning has been problematic since the early 19th century. Moreover, recent evidence suggests it is possible to harness the good will and professional experience of educators without having to punish them (and their teachers) for failing to achieve some standard of performance on any given test (Wilson, Darling-Hammond, & Berry, 2001). Another recent study on the motivational effects of high-stakes testing on low-achieving students concludes that such effects, if they occur, do so (not surprisingly) only under conditions that we already know characterize good teaching and learning. Even so, there are still substantial numbers of students left behind who require additional supports. The authors offer the interpretation that "any set of policies that put the onus on students will fall short in the end" (Roderick & Engle, 2001, p. 221).

A responsible accountability system, therefore, must be built on trust and good will—a bargain, as it were, that educators and students will do their best in exchange for the proper conditions and circumstances within which to do it.

Finally, if we have learned anything from all the research on educational change, it would certainly be that to change institutions and institutional practices is neither simple nor immediate (Fullan, 1991; Goodlad, 1975; Sarason, 1996). Although there may be political urgency to produce quick results, meaningful change comes only from well-developed, deeply integrated social, political, and economic changes generally, and concomitant specific educational changes in commitments, resource allocation, curriculum, instruction, and organizational structures in schools.

All this takes time, a lot of time. Responsible accountability systems will require a long-term focus. Rather than reaching conclusions based on short-term results, a more truly educative paradigm of accountability and change must prevail—a paradigm that is formative and sees multiple forms of information at any point along the way as new evidence that informs present practices and guides even better ones for the future.

CHALLENGING DEEP-ROOTED AXIOMS:
A THOUGHT ADVENTURE

Bringing these beliefs and knowledge-based ideas to bear on schooling practice, particularly in the context of high-stakes accountability, is no easy task. Nonetheless, there are a few schools around the nation that are struggling with alternative assessment and accountability systems (Savich, 2003). One thing is quite apparent, however. Not much can really change by tinkering around with and trying to ameliorate conventional accountability models. We have to challenge ourselves to think out of the box, to identify and seriously question deep assumptions that have led to the current cul-de-sac in traditional accountability practices.

Seymour Sarason has often reminded educators that we labor under axioms or worldviews that are so deeply rooted that they remain both unformulated and unchallenged. For example, Sarason (1983) formulates and challenges the axiom that "education best takes place in classrooms in school buildings" and poses the following question to help start an alternative conversation: "What if it were illegal to teach subject matter in a classroom in a school?"

In a similar vein, we need to challenge our thinking when it comes to truly meaningful alternatives to traditional accountability practices. Another of those unformulated and unchallenged axioms so deeply rooted in educational practice can be formulated thusly: *Accountability for public education must rely on test score information collected from students in sufficiently standardized fashion so that it can be aggregated upward to school, district, state, and national levels.* A corollary axiom is that all this is also necessary so that normative comparisons can be made between individuals, schools, districts, and so forth. Even when standards-based systems are ostensibly criterion-referenced, results are often reported school-by-school in a format that begs for comparative analysis and interpretation.

But let's borrow Sarason's thought-provoking approach and ask: What if it were "against the law" to aggregate and compare student test scores? In other words, we could no longer give students tests for the express purpose of aggregating the results upward and computing means or percentages at, for example, school, district, or state levels. Creating fancy composites of multiple indicators for the purposes of aggregate accountability indexes would also be "illegal."

Now, if you think I've gone off the deep end, you may be right, but your reaction may also indicate how deeply rooted traditional assumptions are about how accountability must be practiced. So let's open up to the possibilities presented by this thought adventure.

Think, for example, of all the problems we might avoid by no longer being obsessed with test-driven accountability and the need to aggregate upward from individual-level information. For example, we would no longer be hamstrung by the need for standardized information. We could open up to possibilities of localizing accountability in responsible ways and tailoring assessment and accountability to the needs of individual students—every individual student.

Moreover, we might rid ourselves of the hegemony of quantitative information (and all the intriguing psychometric problems that need to be solved in making information equivalent), because we would no longer need to worry about what can or cannot be easily aggregated. This, in turn, enables us to think anew and creatively about how to better use and account for the wealth of information—quantitative and qualitative—formally and informally created during the course of teaching and learning. Instead of a multibillion dollar testing and psychometric industry that thrives on solving problems created by the need to standardize, aggregate, and compare, we could invest those dollars and the talents of those psychometricians (along with the talents of expert qualitative analysts) in figuring out new and better ways to accumulate and evaluate student portfolios, assess teaching and learning in the classroom, and so forth. Clearly, both quantitative and qualitative information can be extraordinarily useful for understanding teaching and learning and how any given child is progressing.

A critical consequence of the uncritical acceptance of the aggregation axiom is the failure to honor the professional judgment of educators as a central and critically important feature of any responsible system designed to demonstrate what students know and are able to do. Ultimately, educators should know more about any one child than any test can tell us. And if they worked in organizational and political settings that valued them as professionals and provided the training, resources, and environments necessary to do their work well, good judgments could be made about each and every young person in our schools (Darling-Hammond, 1993; Meier, 1995; Wassermann, 2001).

Assessing students in all sorts of creative and useful ways, therefore, would still be entirely legal and desirable. Some of the current standards-based tests are actually pretty good; they signify better curriculum and higher performance standards for teaching and learning, and good teachers can make good use of these assessment tools *as an on-going part of good instructional practices in the classroom* (Mabry, 1999b; Shepard, 2000). Finding out how well any given student can read, write, think, explain, interpret, communicate, create, problem-solve, collaborate, tolerate, deliberate, compete, invent, evaluate, perform, persist, and so forth, would be essential, especially at the many times when doing such appraisal for a particular student makes sense for that student. This is simply good teaching and learning practice. Accumulating the results of such assessment for any given student tells us much of what we need to know about that student's learning and achievement. By the end of 13 years or so, we should know whether or not that student ought to graduate and get on with his or her life.[3]

Perhaps the most useful outcome of this thought adventure is a reaffirmation of what teachers have known ever since there were teachers: the importance of individualization. Unshackling ourselves from the demands of traditional accountability systems provides wonderful opportunities to think anew about authentic ways in which no child is ever left behind throughout his or her time in public education.

Moreover, this is an invitation not only to revisit useful pedagogical principles such as individualization but also to focus directly on issues of equity. Each and every student has a "learning style," regardless of race, ethnicity, gender, and class, and notwithstanding styles that may have commonalities based on these groupings. Ultimately, to deal fairly with all students is to educate each of them well, recognizing that each brings her or his own individuality plus an educationally rich repertoire of family, cultural, and community experiences (Heckman, 1996). What is crucial is nourishing each and every child's potential to continue to learn, to continue to become.

As Israel Scheffler (1985) so eloquently argues, human potential is not a finite concept. It is not as though a child's potential can be measured in a cup that spills over once it is filled. Helping children "reach their full potential," although a phrase often heard and well-intended, is a statement ill-suited to the true task of education. Children have unlimited potential, or as Scheffler would put it, *capacity, propensity, and capability to become.* The task of political infrastructures and school systems is to create environments within which this is possible. We need to coach and nurture students' on their way to becoming; they are "cups" with infinitely high sides. The last thing we need to do, as educators and as policy makers, is to turn off the tap prematurely on a child or young adult on the basis of information that has little or no predictive validity with respect to the future life prospects of that human being.

Our thought adventure, therefore, leads us to think about each and every child in our schools as special, not just those with "IEPs" (Instructional Educational Programs). One of the many ironies of uncritically accepting the aggregation axiom and traditional test-based accountability systems is the current worry over testing modifications and accommodations for special education students. Our thought adventure, however, suggests that every student deserves "accommodations." A better word for this, of course, would be education. If we were less concerned with test-based indicators and aggregation systems for high-stakes accountability, and more concerned with demonstrating a quality P–12 record of opportunities for and outcomes of learning for each and every student, we would be well on the road to a more responsible accountability system. As noted by Stake (1991) over a decade ago:

> Knowing the rank order of students as to proficiency is not at all the same as knowing what students know. . . . Education is not so much an achieving of some fixed standard. In a true sense, it requires unique and personal definition for each learner. . . . Education is a personal process and a personally unique accomplishment. (cited in Mabry, 1999a, p. 26)

The only way to make sense out of a rhetoric of "leaving no child behind" is to care for and nurture "one kid at a time" (Levine, 2002) — a frame of mind, obviously, that must be applied to each and every student in our public schools.

Toward an Ecology of Responsible Accountability Concepts and Practices

I have proposed some important beliefs, knowledge-based ideas, and a thought adventure to help think less conventionally and more responsibly about accountability practices. These beliefs and claims reinforce, first, the notion of a broad and quality curriculum for all students that generally focuses on the skills and habits of thought requisite for full and participating citizenship in our social and political democracy. Second, they suggest accounting for the whole in ways that do not focus on on-demand, high-stakes tests and the fallout from such practices but do focus, instead, on a broader array of indicators and resource-rich educational environments characterized by all the good conditions and practices known to facilitate better teaching and learning.

This thought adventure has led to reaffirming the importance of individualization and classroom-based information that ought to be naturally accumulated for each student during the formative processes of teaching, learning, and assessment. Each child, adolescent, and young adult needs to be cared for in terms of intellectual, social, personal, and career-oriented educational needs — not to meet some arbitrary level of performance on a high-stakes test, but to develop each person's ability and likelihood "to become." Each has combinations of strengths and weaknesses, and all deserve to thrive in a P–12 educational environment with no test-based threat of failing to graduate hanging over their heads.

Yes, the public has a right to know how well our public schools are educating future citizens, yet, at the same time, those who fashion accountability systems for schooling must themselves be held accountable for doing it responsibly. It is essential that educators not let themselves off the hook when it comes to equity and excellence in our schools and closing the "achievement gap." Yet it is equally essential that the public not let our "educational politicians" off the hook for closing the "rhetorical gap" — the gap between what politicians and policy makers say they want for public education — and mustering the will, commitment, and resources necessary to do something authentic about it.

A responsible "ecology of accountability" (Goodlad, 1979a) must operate on two simultaneous fronts: the day-to-day efforts to improve significantly the education of children in schools, and the concerted efforts of educators and their constituencies to demand that the political infrastructure dramatically alter its priorities and invest the necessary resources where they are needed most to do the job well.

For example, states need to set global educational goals but then fund substantially ongoing professional development and a quality teacher in every classroom, significantly smaller schools and class sizes, and the necessary resources for high-quality learning environments (building, technology, materials, etc.) in *all* schools.

Moreover, states in collaboration with professional educator associations must implement substantive auditing processes that are flexible enough to allow for local variability but yet have enough teeth to identify problematic districts and schools. Several major features should characterize such auditing processes:

- They should be developed collaboratively with educators and their communities and should not be based on high-stakes testing schemes and aggregated data.[4]
- They should be based on coordinated site visitations by teams of educational professionals and public representatives, who are adequately versed in using case-study methods designed to really understand each school.
- They should focus on the school's community, families, and students; its teachers, teaching, and opportunities for learning; its conditions and circumstances (e.g., physical plant, resources, student mobility); its educational goals and means of assessing them; and its information to suggest how well it is doing with respect to each individual student under its care.

Districts and schools need to focus their resources on professional development, teaching, learning, and assessment with particular attention paid to issues of equity and opportunities to learn for all students. Districts and schools also need to work with their local communities to set educational goals and accountability strategies that are comprehensive and meaningful. Real people are involved here; they have real hopes and human desires. These hopes and desires are varied, but there will be remarkable consistency and congruence across schools, districts, and even states (Goodlad, 1979b). And there are good examples over the last decade or so of truly alternative assessment and accountability practices based on the professional judgments of educators, a rich and broad curriculum, and the individual merits of each and every student.[5]

The devil is in the details, of course, but it is a devil worth confronting. It is easy to get pessimistic, even cynical, each time the accountabilist bandwagon makes its rounds onto the educational scene. Yet for the sake of our children and all the good teachers out there, like my friend Andy (see my introduction to this volume), we must keep the conversation going and keep inventing new and promising alternative practices.

January 11, 2003

Dear Andy—

Education needs people like you. And that IS the truth. But not at the peril of your own health or the health of your family—physically, emotionally, economically, or otherwise. I cannot judge the magnitude of these perils for you, or the point at which you ought to decide to just take that job in the private sector that pays three times as much as you're making now as a high school math teacher. Those are personal judgment calls, and calls that you and your family need to make.

I must say, however, that yours is one of the most powerful and compelling sentiments expressed that I have yet read by a teacher—a good teacher—in the trenches of today's schools and the accountability mania facing today's schools. Perhaps what sets you (and others like you) apart from the rest is your sensitivity and insight into the educational policy context within which you struggle. I sometimes—actually more and more now—wonder if I am doing my students any great favors by raising their consciousness to these very same issues, dilemmas, and frustrations. I'm thinking particularly of the students in our programs for preparing future principals, superintendents, and other educational leaders. I worry that I will just reinforce the cynicism and despair that may already be lurking in the hearts and minds of these dedicated educators.

Yet, I worry more about reinforcing acritical and unreflective thinking about whatever ed reform bandwagon and mindless federal (or state) policies are being force-fed to the public schools and to the people who have to live and work and learn in them.

So I guess I come down on the side of critical inquiry in action— unearthing and critiquing the embedded assumptions, beliefs, values, and political interests implicit in "reforms" (present-day "accountabilism," for example)—and trying to be as activist as possible consistent with one's own, reasoned, belief perspectives and willingness to take personal and professional risks. For folks like you and me, this means an always uphill battle, whatever educational organization we're in. But maybe as the quote you shared suggests, we might "do a little" good in the end. Yes, there are personal, social, and economic costs for the decisions we make, and it is important to make good judgments for yourself and your family. There should be no shame attached to whatever the outcomes of these deliberations. And no decision is necessarily forever.

But one decision I know you will make because you can't escape from who you are: Stay intellectually alive; I think that's necessary to stay physically and emotionally healthy. We don't have all the answers, even those of us who think we do. :) I always remember these words from T.S. Eliot (Four Quartets, "Little Gidding"):

> We shall not cease from exploration
> And the end of all our exploring
> Will be to arrive where we started
> And know the place for the first time.

Take care and be good to yourself and your family.

Ken

NOTES

1. Arguably, this ideology can be traced back centuries, long before its commonly assumed origins in Taylorism and scientific management at the turn of the 19th century (Bowers, 1979; Callahan, 1962).

2. See Sirotnik and Kimball (1999); Sirotnik (2002). Much of what follows is taken from the latter source.

3. Keeping track of such information, both qualitative and quantitative,

should be relatively simple in this day and age with computer technology. See, for example, The Learning Record at http://www.learningrecord.org/.

4. If *not* aggregating and reporting data on some type of test battery, standards-based or otherwise, is simply too hard to swallow, politically and/or educationally, then at least consider seriously this alternative to high-stakes testing of individuals: Use matrix sampling, which provides reliable estimates of mean performance at school, district, and state levels using only a fifth to a tenth of the time required for testing at the individual level.

5. Examples: There is much to be learned from the work of the Coalition of Essential Schools and related projects such as ATLAS (Authentic Teaching, Learning, and Assessment for all Students) — their various approaches to exhibiting what students know and can do and to making good professional judgments about student progress (e.g., Cushman, 1996). Ideas for alternative accountability practices can be found in the "accountability toolbox" on the Annenberg Institute for School Reform web site at http://www.annenberginstitute.org/accountability/toolbox/. A related effort with Harvard's Project Zero is the collaborative "Looking at Student's Work" (http://www.lasw.org/index.html). The proposed accountability system for Massachusetts by the Coalition for Authentic Reform of Education (http://www.fairtest.org/arn/masspage.html) includes locally defined authentic assessments, limited standardized testing at parents' discretion, a school audit review process, and annual reporting by districts and schools to parents, the community, and the state. The Nebraska system of accountability is not designed for aggregated comparisons and is based on teachers' professional judgment (Roschewski, 2003). The National Center for Fair and Open Testing (FairTest) has sponsored a number of interesting critiques and useful publications including *Principles and Indicators for Student Assessment Systems* and *Implementing Performance Assessments: A Guide to Classroom, School, and System Reform* (see http://www.fairtest.org).

REFERENCES

Baldwin, J.D., & Baldwin, J.I. (1998). *Behavior principles in everyday life.* Upper Saddle River, NJ: Prentice-Hall.

Barber, B.R. (1993, November). America skips school. *Harper's, 287,* 39–46.

Berlak, H., Newman, F.M., Adams, E., Archbald, D.A., Burgess, T., Raven, J., & Romberg, T. (1992). *Toward a new science of educational testing and assessment.* Albany: State University of New York Press.

Berliner, D.C. (1979). Tempus educare. In P.L. Peterson & H.J. Walberg (Eds.), *Research on teaching: Concepts, findings, and implications* (pp. 120–135). Berkeley, CA: McCutchan.

Bowers, C.A. (1979). The ideological-historical context of an educational metaphor. *Theory Into Practice, 18*(5), 317–322.

Brophy, J.E., & Good, T.L. (1986). Teacher behavior and student achievement. In M.C. Wittrock (Ed.), *Handbook of research on teaching* (pp. 328–375). New York: Macmillan.

Callahan, R.E. (1962). *Education and the cult of efficiency.* Chicago: University of Chicago Press.

Caterall, J.S. (1987, November). On the social costs of dropping out of school. *The High School Journal, 71,* 19–31.

Corno, L., & Snow, R.E. (1986). Adapting teaching to individual differences among learners. In M.C. Wittrock (Ed.), *Handbook of research on teaching* (pp. 605–629). New York: Macmillan.

Cushman, K. (1996, January). Documenting whole-school change in essential schools. *Horace, 12*(3), 1–7.

Darling-Hammond, L. (1993). Reframing the school reform agenda: Developing the capacity for school transformation. *Phi Delta Kappan, 74*(10), 753–761.

Finn, J.D., & Achilles, C.M. (1990). Answers and questions about class size: A statewide experiment. *American Educational Research Journal, 27*(3), 557–577.

Fullan, M.G. (1991). *The new meaning of educational change.* New York: Teachers College Press.

Gardner, H. (1991). *The unschooled mind: How children think and how schools should teach.* New York: Basic Books.

Gay, G. (2000). *Culturally responsive teaching: Theory, research, and practice.* New York: Teachers College Press.

Glass, G.V. (1972). The many faces of educational accountability. *Phi Delta Kappan, 53*(10), 636–639.

Goodlad, J.I. (1975). *The dynamics of educational change.* New York: McGraw-Hill.

Goodlad, J.I. (1979a). An ecological version of accountability. *Theory Into Practice, 18*(5), 309–315.

Goodlad, J.I. (1979b). *What schools are for.* Bloomington, IN: Phi Delta Kappa Educational Foundation.

Goodlad, J.I. (1984). *A place called school: Prospects for the future.* New York: McGraw-Hill.

Goodlad, J.I. (1985). The great American schooling experiment. *Phi Delta Kappan, 67*(4), 266–271.

Gutmann, A. (1987). *Democratic education.* Princeton, NJ: Princeton University Press.

Heckman, P.E. (1996). *The courage to change: Stories from successful school reform.* Thousand Oaks, CA: Corwin Press.

Lessinger, L. (1970). *Every kid a winner: Accountability in education.* New York: Simon and Schuster.

Levine, E. (2002). *One kid at a time: Big lessons from a small school.* New York: Teachers College Press.

Mabry, L. (1999a). *Portfolios plus: A critical guide to alternative assessment.* Thousand Oaks, CA: Corwin Press.

Mabry, L. (1999b). Writing to the rubric: Lingering effects of traditional standardized testing on direct writing assessment. *Phi Delta Kappan, 80*(9), 673–679.

Martin, D.T., Overholt, G.E., & Urban, W.J. (1975). *Accountability in American education: A critique.* Princeton, NJ: Princeton Book Company.

Meier, D. (1995). *The power of their ideas: Lessons from a small school in Harlem.*

Boston: Beacon Press.

National Commission on Teaching and America's Future. (1996). *What matters most: Teaching for America's future.* New York: Author.

No Child Left Behind. (2001). Washington, DC: U.S. Government Printing Office.

Parker, W.C. (2003). *Teaching democracy: Unity and diversity in public life.* New York: Teachers College Press.

Popkewitz, T.S., & Wehlage, G.G. (1973). Accountability: Critique and alternative perspective. *Interchange, 4*(4), 48–62.

Rawls, J. (1971). *A theory of justice.* Cambridge, MA: Belknap Press.

Roderick, M., & Engel, M. (2001). The grasshopper and the ant: Motivational responses of low-achieving students to high-stakes tests. *Educational Evaluation and Policy Analysis, 23*(3), 197–227.

Roschewski, P. (2003). Nebraska STARS line up. *Phi Delta Kappan, 84*(7), 517–520.

Rosenshine, B.V. (1979). Content, time, and direct instruction. IN P.L. Peterson & H.J. Walberg (Eds.), *Research on teaching: Concepts, findings, and implications* (pp. 28–56). Berkeley, CA: McCutchan.

Rumberger, R.W. (2001). *Why students drop out of school and what can be done.* Paper prepared for *Dropouts in America* conference, Harvard University, Cambridge, MA.

Sarason, S.B. (1983). *Schooling in America: Scapegoat or salvation.* New York: Free Press.

Sarason, S.B. (1996). *Revisiting "The culture of school and the problem of change."* New York: Teachers College Press.

Savich, Z. (2003). Prospects for more responsible accountability practices in K-12 schools (Occasional Paper No. 5). Seattle: University of Washington, Institute for the Study of Educational Policy, Project PRAISE.

Scheffler, I. (1985). *Of human potential.* Boston: Routledge & Kegan Paul.

Shepard, L.A. (1991, April). *The effects of high-stakes testing on instruction.* Paper presented at the annual meeting of the American Educational Research Association, Chicago, IL.

Shepard, L.A. (2000). The role of assessment in a learning culture. *Educational Researcher, 29*(7), 4–14.

Shepard, L.A., & Smith, M.L. (Eds.). (1989). *Flunking grades: Research and policies on retention.* London: Falmer Press.

Sidman, M. (1989). *Coercion and its fallout.* Boston: Authors Cooperative.

Sirotnik, K.A. (2002). Promoting responsible accountability in schools and education. *Phi Delta Kappan, 83*(9), 662–673.

Sirotnik, K.A., & Kimball, K. (1999). Standards for standards-based accountability. *Phi Delta Kappan, 81* (3), 209–214.

Soder, R. (2001). Education for democracy: The foundation for democratic character. In R. Soder, J.I. Goodlad, & T.J. McMannon (Eds.), *Developing democratic character in the young* (pp. 182–205). San Francisco: Jossey-Bass.

Stake, R.E. (1991). *The invalidity of standardized testing for measuring mathematics achievement.* Madison: University of Wisconsin, National Center for Research on Mathematical Sciences Education.

Taylor, C. S., & Nolen, S. B. (2004). *Classroom assessment: Supporting teaching and learning in real classrooms.* Englewood Cliffs, NJ: Prentice-Hall.

The Leigh Burstein legacy. (1995). *Educational Evaluation and Policy Analysis.* *17*(3).

Theory Into Practice. (1979). Special issue on accountability, *18*(5).

Wassermann, S. (2001). Quantum theory, the uncertainty principle, and the alchemy of standardized testing. *Phi Delta Kappan, 83*(1), 28–40.

Wheelock, A. (1998). *Safe to be smart: Building a culture for standards-based reform in the middle grades.* Columbus, OH: National Middle School Association.

Wilson, S.M., Darling-Hammond, L., & Berry, B. (2001). *A case of successful teaching policy: Connecticut's long-term efforts to improve teaching and learning.* Seattle, WA: University of Washington, Center for the Study of Teaching and Policy.

About the Editor and the Contributors

Kenneth A. Sirotnik was professor and chair of educational leadership and policy studies, College of Education, University of Washington, Seattle, and director of the college's Institute for the Study of Educational Policy. His research, teaching, and writing ranged widely over many areas and educational policy issues, including methodology of inquiry and evaluation, assessment and accountability, organizational change and school improvement, and teacher and administrator preparation. His most recent book before this, his last, was *Renewing Schools and Teacher Education: An Odyssey in Educational Change* (2001). Ken Sirotnik died on January 29, 2004 at the age of 61, following a brief struggle with cancer.

Nancy Beadie is historian of education and associate professor in educational leadership and policy studies, College of Education, University of Washington, Seattle. Her research focuses on the history of school politics and finance, women in education, and school–community relations. She is coeditor, with Kimberly Tolley, of the recently published *Chartered Schools: Two Hundred Years of Independent Academies in the United States, 1727-1925* (2002). Her current project, *Beyond Human Capital*, is a grassroots history of education and social capital in 19th-century New York.

Gary Blasi is professor of law at the UCLA School of Law. Among his interests are the means by which large organizations and institutions can be made more responsive to those they purport to serve. Examples have included welfare bureaucracies, housing code enforcement agencies, labor law enforcement organizations, and public school systems. A recent article, "Reforming Educational Accountability," examined California's initial efforts at testing-based accountability.

Larry Cuban is professor emeritus of education, Stanford University. His research interests have been the history of reform, teach-

171

ing, and technology in public education. Author of many books on these topics, including the recent work *Why Is It So Hard to Get Good Schools?* (2003), he is currently completing a book on business involvement in school reform in the 20th century.

Linda Mabry is associate professor of education at Washington State University, Vancouver, and an elected member of the boards of directors of the National Center for the Improvement of Educational Assessment and of the American Evaluation Association. She currently chairs an NSF-funded task force to develop a public statement for AEA on the subject of educational accountability. Her publications include *Portfolios Plus: A Critical Guide to Alternative Assessment* (1999) and a recent article on the instructional impact of Washington state's standards-based educational accountability system (2003).

Pedro A. Noguera is Judith K. Dimon Professor of Communities and Schools at the Harvard Graduate School of Education. His research focuses on school responses to social and economic conditions in urban areas. His most recent book, *City Schools and the American Dream: Reclaiming the Promises of Public Education,* was published in 2003.

Jeannie Oakes is Presidential Professor in educational equity and director of UCLA's Institute for Democracy, Education, and Access and University of California's All Campus Consortium on Research for Diversity. Her research examines schooling inequalities and follows the progress of educators and activists seeking socially just schools. Her most recent book, *Becoming Good American Schools: The Struggle for Virtue in Education Reform* (2001), received AERA's Outstanding Book Award.

John Rogers is associate director of UCLA's Institute for Democracy, Education, and Access (IDEA) and the founding editor of IDEA's on-line journal, *Teaching to Change LA.* He studies strategies for engaging urban youth, community members, and teachers as public intellectuals, seeking to make schools places of equal opportunity and democratic life.

Harvey Siegel is professor of philosophy at the University of Miami. His interests are in epistemology, philosophy of science, and philosophy of education. He is the author of many articles in these areas, and of *Relativism Refuted: A Critique of Contemporary Epistemological Relativism* (1987), *Educating Reason: Rationality, Critical Thinking, and Education* (1988), and *Rationality Redeemed?: Further Dialogues on an Educational Ideal* (1997).

Roger Soder is research professor in educational leadership and policy studies, College of Education, University of Washington, Seattle, and vice president of the independent Institute for Educational Inquiry. Soder's research interests continue to focus on rhetoric and leadership, teacher education, administrative transitions, and the role of the university in a free society. His most recent book is *The Language of Leadership* (2001).

Patricia A. Wasley is professor in educational leadership and policy studies and dean of the College of Education at the University of Washington, Seattle. She has recently led a major study of Chicago's small-schools initiative and heads a 5-year national project—"Strengthening and Sustaining Teachers"—which seeks to build sustainable systems of support for teachers. She is lead author of *Kids and School Reform* and has written other books and articles about teachers, students, and school renewal.

Index